Mountain Biking the High Sierra
Guide 3B

Lake Tahoe – North
Tahoe & Toiyabe National Forests
Lake Tahoe Basin Management Unit

by Carol Bonser

Maps and photographs by Carol Bonser
Edited by Réanne and Don Douglass
Cover art by Bill Kelsey

Acknowledgments

The author wishes to thank the following people for their help and support throughout the creation of this guidebook. Mike Peart, who willingly explored with me the miles of trails described in this book, my brother, Gordon, who kept my mountain bike running for another summer of riding in the Sierra, and the rest of my family for their continued support. Thanks to all the "Sunday Riders" who have continued to support our ride program and offer encouragement to finish this second book. Special thanks to those of you whom Mike and I met out on the trail who shared with us some of your favorite rides so that others can enjoy them too. And last, thanks to Don and Réanne Douglass for asking me to write *Guide 3B* and supplying the extra motivation I needed to finish it, and to Sue Irwin for her help in readying the manuscript.

Important Disclaimer

Mountain biking is a potentially dangerous sport in which serious injury and death can and do occur. Trails have numerous natural and man made hazards, and conditions may change constantly. Most of the routes in this book are not signed or patrolled. This book may contain errors and omissions and is not a substitute for proper instruction, experience and preparedness.

You must accept full and complete responsibility for yourself while bicycling. The authors, editors, publishers, land manager, distributors, retailers and others associated with this book are not responsible for errors or omissions and do not accept liability for any loss or damage incurred from using this book.

ISBN 0-938665-07-3

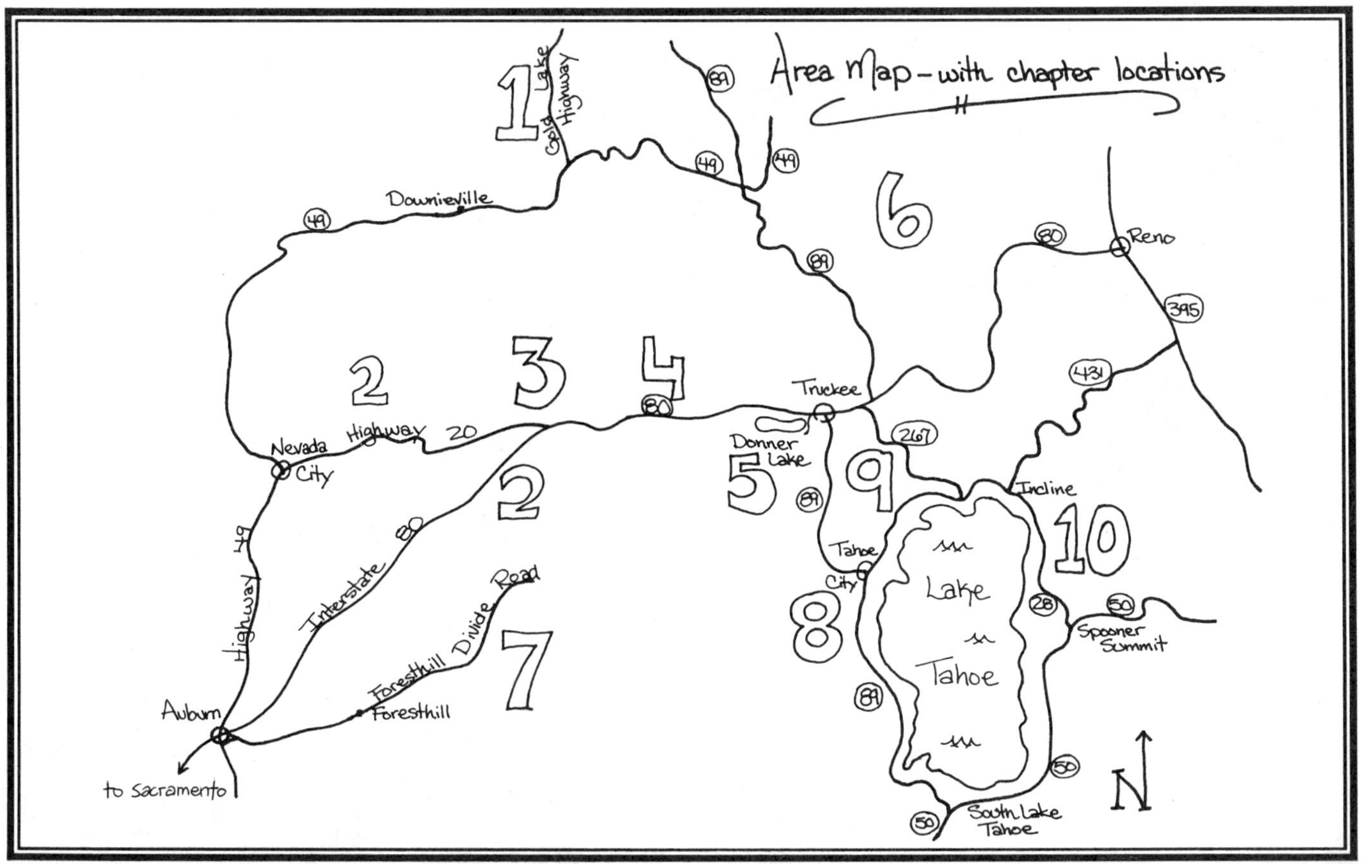

Area Map - with chapter locations #
1
Gold Lake Highway
89
49
49
Downieville
49
6
80
Reno
395
431
2
3
4
Truckee
80
267
Donner Lake
Nevada Highway 20
Nevada City
5
89
9
Incline
2
10
Highway 49
Interstate 80
Tahoe City
28
50
Foresthill Divide Road
8
Lake
Spooner Summit
7
Tahoe
89
Foresthill
Auburn
50
to Sacramento
50
South Lake Tahoe
N

TABLE OF CONTENTS

Chapter 1 Sierra Buttes 11
Map 1 – Lakes Basin: Upper Sardine Lake; Mills Peak Lookout; Haskell Peak Loop; Frazier Falls Picnic Ride; Summit Lake; Round Lake Loop; Downieville Downhill; Sierra Buttes Lookout

Chapter 2 The Foothills 21
Map 2 – Emigrant Gap: Sailor Point Loop; Sawtooth Ridge Loop; Helester Point; Onion Valley/Sailor Point
Map 3 – Malakoff Diggings: Relief Hill Loop; Martin Ranch

Chapter 3 Interstate 80 Corridor – Bowman Lake 27
Map 4 – Carr Lake Trailhead: Shotgun Lake; Island Lake Loop; Glacier Lake
Map 4 – Jackson Creek Campground: Faucherie Lake; Canyon Creek; Bowman, Weaver & McMurray Lakes; Meadow Lake
Eagle Mountain Bike Park

Chapter 4 Interstate 80 Corridor – Cisco Grove 35
Map 5 – Indian Springs Trailhead: Eagle Lakes/Fordyce Bridge; Spaulding Lake; Signal Peak Hill Climb; Fordyce OHV Trail to Meadow Lake
Map 5 – Sterling Lake / Glacier Basin Area: Cisco Grove to Lake Sterling or Fordyce Lake; Glacier Lakes Basin Loop; Mossy Pond Loop

Chapter 5 Donner Lake 43
Map 6 – Donner Memorial State Park: Tinkers Knob Loop; Coldstream Valley; Lakeview Canyon Loop; Old Emigrant Trail to Donner Peak

Chapter 6 Stampede / Sardine Peak 49
Map 7 – Stampede Reservoir: North Shore; Sardine Peak Lookout Loop; Sardine Valley Loop
Map 8 – Bear Valley Campground: Sardine Peak Lookout from Bear Valley; Western Juniper Loop; Bear Valley; Turner Canyon Loop

IMBA Rules of the Trails

1. Ride on open trails only.   4. Always yield trail.
2. Leave no trace.   5. Never spook animals.
3. Control your bicycle!   6. Plan ahead.

These volunteer non-profit organizations need your help:

Tahoe Area Mountain Bicycling Association (TAMBA)
P.O. Box 1488, Tahoe City, CA 95730   916-525-5100

International Mountain Bicycling Association (IMBA)
P.O. Box 412043, Los Angeles, CA 90041   818-792-8830

Special Considerations

Guide 3B covers the Tahoe National Forest, parts of the Toiyabe National Forest and the northern portion of the Lake Tahoe Basin Management Unit. The National Forest within this area starts in the foothills at 2,000 feet, rising to nearly 10,000 in the mountains with wide ranges in climate and weather conditions.

This guide book does not show all of the rides within each area. Part of the fun is discoveries you make while on the trail. Ride with your eyes wide open all the time!

1. **Courtesy.** Know and follow the IMBA Rules of the Trail (see the Appendix). Extend courtesy to all other trail users and follow the golden rule. The trails and roads in these areas are used by fishermen, hunters, loggers and hikers, who all feel proprietary about the use of the trails. Mountain bikes are newcomers.

2. **Preparations.** Plan your trip carefully by developing a check list. Know your abilities and your equipment. Prepare to be self-sufficient at all times. If you plan to camp, be sure to read the warnings at the beginning of the chapters. Many of the campgrounds shown on the Tahoe National Forest are "undeveloped sites" which means that treated drinking water may not be available. Bring gallons of water with you from home to reduce the amount of stream water you'll have to treat (boiled for five minutes or filtered) before you can drink it.

3. **Mountain Conditions.**
   •Sun: Many of the high country rides travel over granite rocks which, in terms of reflected light, you can compare to riding across a snowfield. Protect your skin against the sun's harmful rays. Use sunscreen with a rating of 15 or more.
   Don't forget your eyes! Wear sunglasses with 100 UV protection. Clear lenses are also available with 100 UV protection. Avoid glass lenses!
   •Low Humidity: Start each trip with a minimum of 2 full water bottles, or more. Gallons of water may not be sufficient for really hot weather. Force yourself to drink, whether or not you feel thirsty. Untreated drinking water may cause Giardiasis or other diseases. Carry water from a known source, or treat it.
   •Variations in Temperature: Never travel to the high country without being prepared for afternoon thundershowers. It is not uncommon to get a brief hailstorm in mid-summer! Carry extra clothing – a windbreaker, gloves, stocking cap, and use the multi-layer system so you can adjust according to conditions. Keep an eye on changing cloud and wind conditions.
   •Wind: Wind can deplete your energy. Sluggish or cramping muscles and fatigue indicate the need for calories. Carry high-energy snack foods such as granola bars, dried fruits and nuts to maintain strength and warmth, and add clothing layers as the temperature drops or the wind increases.
   •Know how to deal with dehydration, hypothermia, altitude sickness, sunburn or heatstroke. Be sensitive at all times to the natural environment – the land can be frightening and unforgiving. If you break down, it may take you longer to walk out than it took you to ride in! Check with your local Red Cross, Sierra Club, or mountaineering textbooks for detailed survival information.

4. **Horses and Pack Animals.** Many of the trails mentioned in this guide are used by recreational horse riders. Some horses are spooked easily, so make them aware of your presence well in advance of the encounter.

If you come upon horses moving toward you, yield the right-of-way, even when it seems inconvenient. Carry your bike to the downhill side and stand quietly, well off the trail in a spot where the animals can see you clearly. A startled horse can cause serious injuries both to an inexperienced rider and to itself.

If you come upon horses moving ahead of you in the same direction, stop well behind them. Do not attempt to pass until you have alerted the riders and asked for permission. Then, pass as quietly as you can on the downhill side of the trail. It is *your* responsibility to ensure that such encounters are safe for everyone!

5. **Respect the Environment.** Minimize your impact on the natural environment. *Remember, mountain bikes are not allowed in Wilderness Areas, on the Pacific Crest Trail and in certain other restricted areas.* Ask, when in doubt. You are a visitor. Leave plants and animals alone; historic and cultural sites untouched. Stay on established roads and trails, and do not enter private property. Follow posted instructions and use good common sense. *Note:* If you plan to camp within the National Forest, you need a Campfire Permit to have a fire or use a stove outside of a campground. For information on permits, regulations and seasonal fire closures, contact the Tahoe National Forest Service at (916) 265-4531.

6. **Control and Safety.** Control your mountain bike at all times. Guard against excessive speed. Avoid overheated rims and brakes on long or steep downhill rides. Lower your center of gravity by lowering your seat on downhills. Lower your tire pressure on rough or sandy stretches. Avoid opening weekend of hunting season. Carry first aid supplies and bike tools for emergencies.

7. **First Aid and Safety.** Carry first aid for your body as well as for your bike. If you have allergies be sure to bring your medicine, whether it's for pollen or bee stings. Sunscreen saves your skin. Bring bandages and ointment for cuts and scrapes, and aspirin for those aches that won't go away. Lightweight cord is handy for tourniquets or splints. A warning about things that can hurt you:

There are *black bears* out and about. Food seems to cause the most problems, so a clean camp is advised. *Rattlesnakes* can be startling and are dangerous at close range, but they are usually noisy and retreat readily. Snakes are most often seen in the lower elevations, close to a water source, hidden in the rocks. Most snake bites are reported in April, May and early June when the snakes lie in the sun trying to warm up. Later on in the summer, they will be hiding in the shade, and you probably won't see them. *Mosquitoes and deerflies* are more of an annoyance than a true health hazard. If the mosquitoes like you, carry insect repellant when riding, especially during the months of May through July. Avoid *poison oak.* Usually found in this area at 4,000 feet and below, this three-leaved plant – sometimes a bush, sometimes a vine – has an oil that causes rashes with blistering one to five days after contact. Avoid direct contact with any part of the plant, contact with an animal that's brushed against it, contact with clothing or gloves that have touched it, or inhalation of smoke from a burning plant. Wash immediately to prevent or lessen the rash. For more severe cases see your doctor. Extremely sensitive people check about having desensitizing shots. *Crashes:* Most crashes don't cause serious injury. Stay under control and slow for the unexpected. Wear protective gear — helmet, full-fingered leather gloves, over-the-ankle boots, long pants, long sleeves and dark glasses to protect against scrapes and impacts with rocks, dirt, and brush.

8. **Maps & Navigation.** Everyone who enjoys exploring by mountain bike should know how to read a map and use a compass.The maps in this book are designed to be used with National Forest Maps and U.S. Geological Survey Maps (USGS topo maps). A "legal description" (location) is given for the starting point of each area. For example, T20N, R16E, Section 30 is the location of the Bear Valley Campground, a good place to camp and ride. Maps are made up of grids. Across the top and bottom of the Tahoe National Forest Map are the numbers R8E to R18E, for Range 8 East to Range 18 East. Vertically on the left and right are T13N to T22N, for Township 13 North to Township 22 North. Using the legal description for Bear Valley Campground, find where T20N and R16E cross, forming a large square made up of smaller squares, called sections. Each section is numbered from 1-36. You should now have no problem locating Capp's Crossing within Section 30. *Warning: Not all the roads on the USFS maps are on the guidebook maps, and not all the roads found on the maps in this guidebook are on the USFS maps!*

The handiest maps to use while riding are the USGS topo maps, 7.5 minute series. These maps tend to be the most recent and have many of the newer roads on them. Everything you learned about the legal descriptions is the same for the topo maps, the squares are just larger. Each section of the maps, no matter which one you are using, represents one square mile.

Another hint! Have you ever noticed trees in the forest with yellow tags nailed onto them? These tags are called K-Tags. On each K-Tag is one complete Township with 36 sections. On the top or bottom of the tag will be the Township and Range numbers. Then there should be one nail hole in a section square indicating the section you're in. Look on your map and you can quickly find out where you are!

It's easy to get lost. Before you leave on a trip, tell someone where you're going, when you expect to return, and what to do in case you don't return on time. When you are more than six hours overdue ask them to contact the appropriate County Sheriff's Department, giving full details about your vehicle and your trip plans. En route, keep track of your position on your trip map(s); record the time you arrive at a known point on the map. Look back frequently in the direction from which you came, in case you need to retrace your path. Don't be afraid to turn back when conditions change or if the going is rougher than you expected. In case of emergency while you're in this area, dial 911.

9. **Trailside Bike Repair.** Minimum equipment: pump, spare tube, patches, 2 tubes of patch glue, 6" adjustable wrench, Allen wrenches, chain tool, spoke wrench, and spare axle. Tools may be shared with others in your group.

Correct inflation, wide tires, and avoiding rocks will prevent most flats. Those same rocks cause bent and broken axles. Grease, oil, and proper adjustment will prevent almost all mechanical failures. Frequent stream crossings wash out chain grease; carry extra or, use a banana peel!

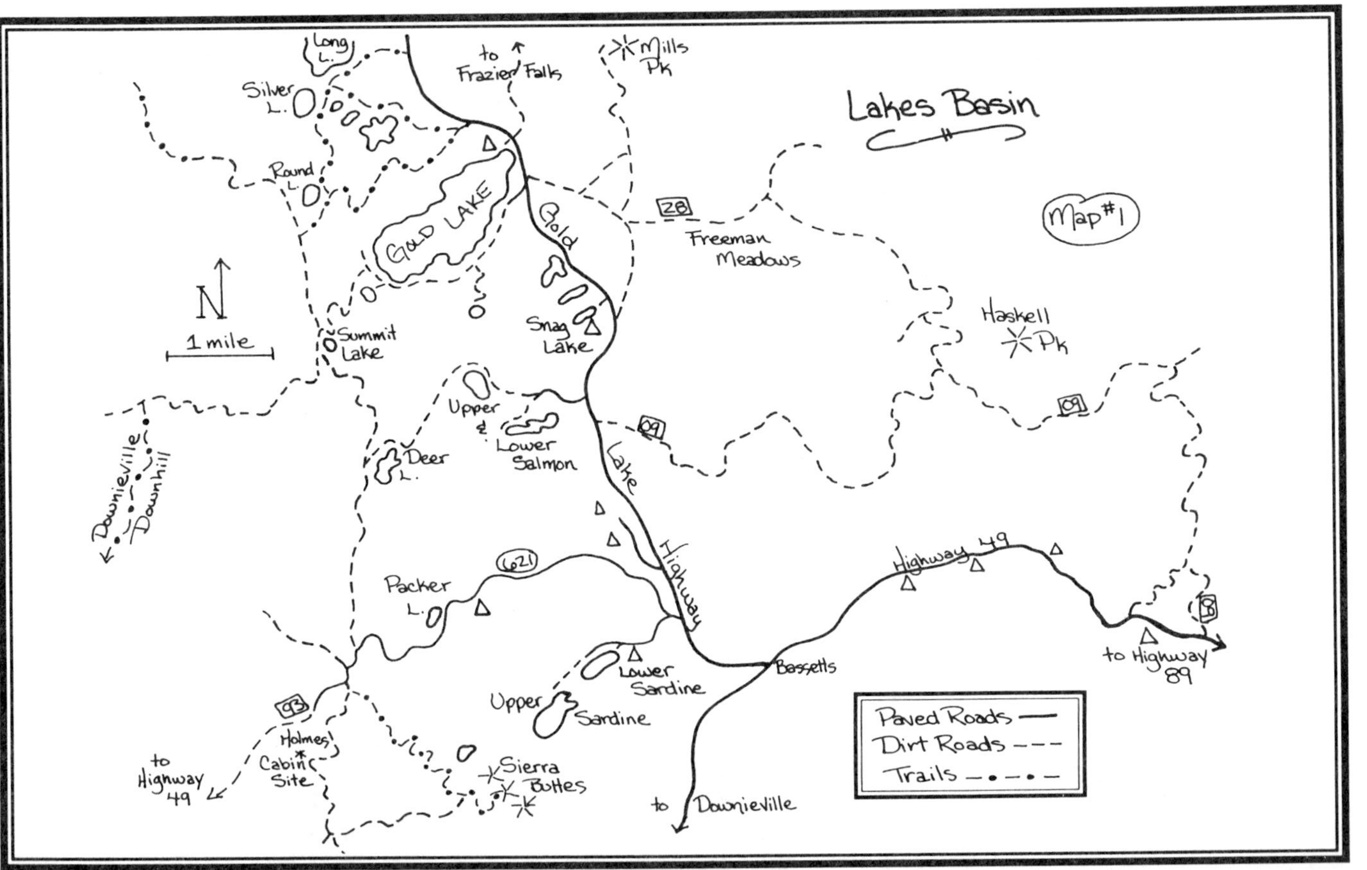

Lakes Basin
Map #1
Long L.
Silver L.
Round L.
to Frazier Falls
Mills Pk
Gold LAKE
Gold
28
Freeman Meadows
Haskell Pk
N
1 mile
Summit Lake
Snag Lake
Upper & Lower Salmon
Deer L.
Lake
Highway
Packer L.
621
Highway 49
Downieville Downhill
Lower Sardine
Upper Sardine
Bassetts
to Highway 89
93
Holmes Cabin Site
to Highway 49
Sierra Buttes
to Downieville
Paved Roads
Dirt Roads
Trails

CHAPTER 1   SIERRA BUTTES
Upper Sardine Lake; Mills Peak Lookout; Haskell Peak Loop;
Frazier Falls Picnic Ride; Summit Lake; Round Lake Loop;
Downieville Downhill; Sierra Buttes Lookout

A visit to Sierra Buttes should appear on every mountain bike riders "must do" list! The Sierra Buttes are gigantic, jagged, rocky pinnacles that push straight up over 2,000 feet from the surrounding forest lands. They can be seen from miles away and form a strong contrast to the more gentle northern Sierra Nevada. The forest land below the Buttes, known as the Lakes Basin Recreation Area, has an incredible amount of area to explore by mountain bike. Nearby lakes provide swimming, fishing, windsurfing and water skiing and there are many places to camp. Plan to spend at least three days, but you won't be disappointed if you take an entire week's vacation here.

Sierra Buttes and the Lakes Basin are located on the Gold Lake Highway, named after Gold Lake, the largest lake in the area. *From the Bay Area or Sacramento:* Take Interstate 80 east to Auburn and go north on Highway 49. Highway 49 travels through the Gold Country and then begins to climb back into the Sierra Nevada. About 16 miles east of Downieville, at the small town of Bassetts, turn north on the Gold Lake Highway. *From Lake Tahoe:* Go north on Highway 89 to Sierraville. Turn left, staying on Highway 89 (49 and 89 at this point), and follow the signs to Quincy. Five miles farther turn left on Highway 49 and follow the signs to Downieville. You will drive over Yuba Pass before dropping down the west side to get your first glimpse of the Sierra Buttes. When you reach Bassetts, turn right (north) on the Gold Lakes Highway.

About the Rides: The rides in this chapter all start from different campgrounds or intersections along Gold Lake Highway. You can either drive to the starting points, or look at the map to see how much pavement riding is involved from your campsite to the start. The Pacific Crest Trail (closed to mountain bikes) runs north-south along the edge of this area. Fortunately, there are plenty of 4-wheel drive roads that follow the trail, so this closure doesn't cause much of a problem in planning your rides.

Emergency: Dial 911. Sierra County Sheriff: (916) 289-3234. US Forest Service, Downieville Ranger District: (916) 288-3231. Pay phones are located at Bassetts and Sardine Lake Resort.

Campgrounds: Sardine and Salmon Creek are full-service USFS campgrounds with water, tables, fire rings and vault toilets. There are also five camping areas that the Forest Service calls "undesignated" or "undeveloped" campgrounds. These all have vault toilets, but they may or may not have tables and they probably offer only stream or lake water for drinking. All water from these areas should be boiled or filtered before drinking. Due to the popularity of this region, camping is primarily limited to the campgrounds.

Seasons: June through October.

Nearest Services: There is a store and a gas station in Bassetts, but you should bring the majority of your supplies from home. The nearest bike shops are in

Truckee or Grass Valley – both a few hours away – so bring all your tools and extra bike parts.

In addition to camping, there are cabins for rent at Sardine Lakes Resort. These are old wooden structures that have been refurbished, and Sardine Lakes Resort is a small, beautiful resort to visit on your tour. Boats can be rented, and there is a Dining Room that serves delicious gourmet family-style dinners (a great treat after a hard day of riding!). For more information on Sardine Lake Resort, call (916) 862-1196.

LAKES BASIN

Ride #1 - Upper Sardine Lake

Topo Maps: Haypress Valley and Sierra City 7.5 min., or Sierra City 15 min. Ride starts at T20N, R12E, Section 3.
Level of Difficulty: Short intermediate level ride. The road is rough and rocky; beginners may prefer to walk. But don't miss this one, even if you hike instead of ride. The view is worth the effort it takes to get there!
Mileage: 2.5 miles out and back.
Elevation: 5,700 ft. to 6,000 ft.

The Ride: 0.0 mile – From Sardine Lake Campground, ride southwest towards Lower Sardine Lake and go past the picnic area to the entrance of Sardine Lake Resort. Turn right on the dirt road that is just to the right of the resort. Follow the rocky, dirt road 1 mile farther up to Upper Sardine Lake. On the way up you will be treated to a view down to Lower Sardine Lake with the Sierra Buttes in the background. But the view gets even better when you get to Upper Sardine Lake where the Buttes rise 2,500 feet straight up from the water! Be sure to search for the lookout tower perched on the rocks. Upper Sardine Lake is a fun place for an early morning or early evening ride. Plan to spend some time just enjoying the sights.

Ride #2 - Mills Peak Lookout

Topo Maps: Gold Lake and Clio 7.5 min., or Sierra City 15 min. Ride starts at T12N, R12E, Section 16.
Level of Difficulty: Most beginners in good physical condition could handle this one. With only 900 feet of elevation gain, this is an easy ride compared to most lookout hill climbs.
Mileage: 7.6 miles out and back.
Elevation: 6,400 ft. to 7,300 ft.

The Ride: 0.0 mile – From the Gold Lake camping area, go south on Gold Lake Highway. 0.6 mile – Turn left on the dirt road with a sign that reads: *Mills Peak Lookout 3 1/4 miles.* 1.3 miles – Ignore a road that enters from the left. 1.6 miles – Turn left here. You are passing through private land, so stay on the main road. As you leave the private land, the road begins to climb and makes the final ascent to the lookout. There are several junctions, but just stay on the main road which continues uphill. 3.8 miles – From the top you can see Mohawk Valley in the distance to the northeast, the high point of Mills Peak to the southeast, and the jagged pinnacles of Sierra Buttes to the southwest. When you have finished exploring follow your tracks back, enjoying the downhill. For a longer loop see Ride #3 below.

Ride #3 - Haskell Peak Loop

Topo Maps: Gold Lake and Clio 7.5 min., or Sierra City 15 min. Ride starts at T12N, R12E, Section 16 (Gold Lake) or Section 21 (Snag Lake).
Level of Difficulty: Strong beginners and up. Suitable for all riders who have the endurance to ride the distance. All of the road surfaces are either good dirt or gravel, so this is not technical.
Mileage: 17 miles round trip from Snag Lake; 18.5 miles round trip from Gold Lake.
Elevation: 6,400 ft. to 7,720 ft.
Water: Carry all you think you will need. You will pass a few creeks along the way, but I would not count on them as a year-round source. Be sure to filter or treat all water you take from mountain streams.

The Ride: 0.0 mile – From Gold Lake camping area, follow the directions in Ride #2 for the first 1.6 miles. Then, instead of turning towards the lookout you continue straight ahead and shortly arrive at an intersection (1.7 miles). Head straight on Forest Road 28.

Optional Start: From Snag Lake Campground, go right on Gold Lake Highway for 0.2 mile. Turn left on the road to Mills Peak and continue to an intersection 0.8 mile farther (1.0 miles total). Turn right onto Forest Road 28. If you take this option, be sure to adjust your mileage by subtracting 0.7, since all figures are given from here on for the trip starting at Gold Lake.

Once you are on Forest Road 28 (1.7 miles from Gold Lake or 1.0 miles from Snag Lake), follow the signs to Church Meadows and Haskell Peak. 2.3 miles. – Turn right at the road signed: *Dead End Road, Not Maintained 12N11, Church Creek Meadows.* You will ride past large Freeman Meadow, with Church Creek running through it. 3.9 miles – Stay left at the intersection. The road begins to gradually climb. 4.1 miles – At another intersection, continue straight ahead. From here on you will pass several intersections, but just remember to stay on the main road that climbs to the saddle just west of Haskell Peak. 6.3 miles – The climbing is over and you are on the saddle. As you turn the corner you get a good look at the rocky top of Haskell Peak (elev. 8,107 ft.). You can detour over to the base of the rocks, but I think you will have to hike to get to the top of the peak. After you've enjoyed the view, prepare yourself for the next eight miles – almost all downhill! 6.8 miles – Continue down the main road to the three-way intersection. 7.1 miles – Turn left.

8.2 miles – Turn right and continue downhill. From here the road begins to wind its way around the ridge. You climb a little and then head downhill. The road is now marked *Forest Road 09,* and it has arrows and orange diamonds denoting a ski and snowmobile route. Stay on Forest Road 09, and you should have no problem keeping to the route even though there are logging roads everywhere! Watch for indications of active logging, and ride with caution. 12.3 miles – You cross Howard Creek and then have to climb a bit. Winding around the ridge, you are treated to another great view of Sierra Buttes in the distance. From here it is all downhill to Gold Lake Highway. 15.2 miles – At Gold Lake Highway turn right and ride back to your starting point – 1.6 miles to Snag Lake or 3.3 miles to Gold Lake.

Ride #4 - Frazier Falls Picnic Ride
Topo Maps: Gold Lake 7.5 min., or Sierra City 15 min. Ride starts at T12N, R12E, Section 16.
Level of Difficulty: Easy. The ride out and back to Frazier Falls is suitable for families with children or those looking for a short ride and a good place to picnic. It is about as flat as a mountain bike ride can be, with only 200 feet of elevation change. The longer loop is still an easy ride but not recommended for children because you have to ride on the Gold Lake Highway for 1.8 miles.
Mileage: 3.6 miles; loop ride 5.4 miles.
Elevation: 6,200 ft. to 6,400 ft. Longer loop 6,200 ft. to 6,500 ft.

The Ride: 0.0 mile – From the Gold Lake camping area, ride out to Gold Lake Highway. Look across the highway for a dirt road; ride across when it is safe and continue out the dirt road. The ride is slightly downhill as you make your way past rocky outcroppings and small meadows. 1.8 miles – You arrive at the Frazier Falls trailhead and picnic area. Park your bike and take the short hike over to the falls. Enjoy your picnic, then ride back to Gold Lake for a swim.

For the longer loop, you can continue on the main road, turn left at 2.5 miles and tie back into Gold Lake Highway. 3.6 miles – Turn left onto the highway and ride back to Gold Lake. This is a nice loop, but it is almost all on paved roads!

Ride #5 - Summit Lake
Topo Maps: Gold Lake 7.5 min., or Sierra City 15 min. Ride starts at T12N, R12E, Section 16.
Level of Difficulty: Intermediate because of the technical rocky sections. Beginners can do part of the ride – out to Little Gold Lake and back – to practice on the rocks.
Mileage: 8 miles to Summit Lake and back, 10 miles if you detour to all of the other lakes.
Elevation: 6,407 ft. to 7,000 ft.
Water: The nearest treated water is back at Salmon Creek Campground. Be sure to filter or treat all water you take from lakes and streams.

The Ride: 0.0 mile – From the Gold Lake camping area, turn right (south) onto Gold Lake Highway. 0.8 mile – Turn right on the gravel road that goes to the Pack Station and the boat launching area. There is a dirt route connecting the camping

area to the boat launch, but we found the short ride on the pavement a good way to warm up for the next section of the ride. 1.2 miles – Ride past the turn-off to the stable and the boat ramp, and continue to the end of the gravel road. Look to your left for a sign: *Squaw Lake 1 mile - Little Gold Lake 2 miles - Summit Lake 3 miles.* From here on the road gets rough! Some sections are quite rocky and look like streambeds, but never for very long. Be on the lookout for horses, because the Pack Station runs five trips a day on busy weekends. The horses seem accustomed to mountain bikes, but don't forget that the riders have very little experience. If you see a group of horseback riders, slow down to a snail's pace or dismount until they pass.

2.0 miles – On your left is the turn-off to Squaw Lake, about a half a mile uphill (250 feet elevation gain). Detour up to the lake now, or stop on your way back. (The mileage given below does not include any of these lake detours.) 2.7 miles – On your left is the turn-off to Little Gold Lake, which you can see through the trees. 3.0 miles – Ride southeast to the far end of Gold Lake to some great campsites. Continue until you reach the *Private Land* sign and the cable across the road. Take a left turn, and begin the uphill part of the ride. The next section winds up and away from Gold Lake, passing a cabin, then crosses the Pacific Crest Trail. Stay on the main road to the top of the ridge – a good climb.

If you start to tire or have to push your bike, just remember that it is only 1 mile to the top. After you crest the ridge the road goes downhill to Summit Lake. 4.0 miles – You have reached the end of this ride. Summit Lake is off to the left, and you are at a major OHV Trail intersection. A right turn heads to Round Lake (see Ride #6); a left turn leads to Deer Lake and on out the ridge towards the Buttes. The road straight ahead takes you on the Downieville Downhill, Ride #7. When you are through exploring, either follow the directions for Ride #6, or turn around and enjoy a fast downhill back to Gold Lake!

Ride #6 - Round Lake Loop
Topo Maps: Gold Lake 7.5 min., or Sierra City 15 min. Ride starts at T12N, R12E, Section 16.
Level of Difficulty: Intermediate or better. This is a scenic ride for people who don't mind pushing their bikes through some of the rough spots. Be prepared for a mile of steady climbing, rocky sections and some single-track.
Mileage: 9 miles.
Elevation : 6,400 ft. to 7,320 ft.

The Ride: 0.0 mile – Start from Gold Lake camping area and follow the directions for Ride # 5 for the first 4 miles to Summit Lake. 4.0 miles – Turn right at the intersection. The road climbs a bit more before you reach an open ridge with a great view of Gold Lake. The OHV road you are riding crosses the Pacific Crest Trail in several places. 5.3 miles – Turn right, staying on the east side of the ridge. (The road to the left goes to Oakland Pond.) A short distance farther you pass a sign: *Round Lake 3/4 mile - Silver Lake 1 3/4 mile - Lakes Basin Campground 2 3/4 mile.* 6.0 miles – On the edge of the ridge you are treated to a view of Round

Lake and Long Lake, with Mt. Elwell in the background. The next section is a steep downhill that many prefer to walk.

6.2 miles – You arrive at the overlook above Round Lake. There is a plaque that tells about a 400-foot mine shaft that was dug here shortly before World War I, when the ore was valued at $1.05 a ton! It is hard to believe that there was that much activity at such a remote place as this, so long ago. This spot is also the intersection with the trail to Silver Lake. From this point you should pull out your map and plan the rest of your journey. There are trails and old roads connecting all of the lakes. A nice loop option is to ride out to Silver Lake, Cub Lake, Little Bear Lake, Big Bear Lake, and then tie into the road on the Round Lake Loop.

To complete the Round Lake Loop, continue on the main trail that turns into a narrow old road. Around the corner you pass an old shelter, and then the road starts downhill. This next section is a lot of fun as you go through rocky areas and back into the forest. Be on the lookout for hikers. The roadbed is wide enough to pass them safely, but be sure to let them know you are coming. 7.5 miles – The old road intersects with the trail to Bear Lakes. (This is where you will re-enter if you take the optional ride out to the other lakes.) 7.8 miles – The old road ends at a trailhead parking area. There is a good map of the Lakes Basin area that you may want to look at if you don't have a topo map. Ride out to Gold Lakes Highway, turn right, and continue back to Gold Lake.

Ride # 7 - Downieville Downhill
This is a ride we heard about from a group of riders we met while exploring the area. Unfortunately we were unable to do the entire ride because it requires a shuttle. The following directions are from the riders we met and from topo maps. If you do the ride, take the 7.5 min. USGS topo maps along and you should have no problem finding your way to Downieville. You will need to arrange a shuttle or leave a car somewhere near the town of Downieville. There is very little parking in Downieville, so you might find it easier to have someone meet you just outside of town along Highway 49. (There are good swimming holes on the North Fork of the Yuba River.)

Topo Maps: Gold Lake, Sierra City and Downieville 7.5 min. are the best. Otherwise use Sierra City and Downieville 15 min. maps.
Level of Difficulty: Experienced riders only. Losing over 4,000 feet of elevation can be exhilarating, but it is also tiring. Be sure you have a good bike with a decent set of brakes.
Mileage: 16 miles one way.
Elevation: 6,407 ft. to 7,000 ft. to 2,899 ft.
Water: This ride takes you along several creeks. Be sure to filter or treat all water you take from the streams.

The Ride: 0.0. mile – From Gold Lake camping area, follow Ride #5 the first 4 miles to Summit Lake. 4.0 miles – When you reach Summit Lake continue on the main OHV trail that goes straight ahead. Follow the signs to Gold Valley and

Pauley Trail. (On some maps this road is called the Summit Lake Trail.) As you drop down the west side of the ridge, it's an all downhill ride into Gold Valley 1,100 feet below. You ride past several intersections, many of them leading to old mines. Stay on the main road and keep following the signs to Gold Valley and Pauley Trail. 7.2 miles – When you enter Gold Valley, the road turns south down the valley. After crossing Pauley Creek, you arrive at an intersection with the road going to Smith Lake, which is located 0.7 mile west of this point. Continue to the southern end of Gold Valley on the Pauley Creek Trail. 7.7 miles – As you leave the valley, the trail descends quickly into Pauley Creek Canyon. Continue on the trail as it follows the creek downstream.

9.4 miles – Pauley Creek Trail intersects with Butcher Ranch Trail (11E08). Stay to the right and continue to follow Pauley Creek. You have now lost over 2,000 feet in elevation since you left Summit Lake, and the canyon walls are getting quite steep. Continue on the main trail that goes downhill. 11.4 miles – Stay to the right on the Third Divide Trail (11E07). Ride through the divide and continue downhill to Lavezzola Creek and Empire Ranch. Stay left on the main road that follows Lavezzola Creek, crosses it, and goes through the Second Divide back to Pauley Creek. From here just stay on the main road and follow all the signs to Downieville. Eventually you will be on road S514. 14.8 miles – When the dirt road ends, continue straight ahead on the paved road that takes you into Downieville. 15.6 miles – Turn left onto Highway 49. Hopefully you will be able to find your car!

Ride #8 - Sierra Buttes Lookout

Topo Maps: Sierra City 7.5 min. or 15 min. Ride starts in T20N, R12E, Section 5.
Level of Difficulty: A difficult ride for advanced riders who like the challenge of a steep hill climb. Others may prefer to hike up the PCT, instead.
Mileage: 16 miles out and back from Packer Lake; 7.5 miles out and back from to Holmes Cabin.
Elevation: 6,224 ft. to 8,591 ft. from Packer Lake; 6,773 ft. to 8,591 ft. from Holmes Cabin Site.
Water: None. Carry all you will need.

Most mountain bike riders think of lookouts as destination points for ultimate hill climbs and wild descents, and the Sierra Buttes Lookout is one of the toughest around. From the lakes below, you can see the Lookout Tower perched on the top of the highest pinnacle. This is not a route recommended for those afraid of heights. Once you arrive at the top of the road, you have three flights of steep narrow stairs (with guard rails!) to climb before reaching the tower. ***Caution: Do not attempt to ride to the Sierra Buttes Lookout Tower unless you have good brakes! The Downhill is steep, and the drop-offs are severe!*** Some people prefer to walk up to the lookout rather than ride (push) up the OHV road to the top.

Going to Sierra Buttes Lookout is something everyone should do who has more than one day to spend in this area. To get to the trailhead follow the signs to Packer Lake. Ride or drive past Packer Lake on Forest Road 93. The road is paved, although quite narrow all the way to the top (suitable for mountain bikes, but not road bikes!).

From the top, turn left and follow the signs to the Lookout. Stay on the main road and you will arrive at the Pacific Crest Trailhead, which is also the trailhead for the Lookout. If you decide to hike to the top, park your bikes here. (I would carry locks for stashing them behind trees somewhere.) Continue on by foot. If you to ride to the lookout continue on the gravel road that will take you to the OHV road to the top.

From here the road goes downhill and winds its way around the ridge. In the big left turn that goes around the ridge, you will see the old Holmes Cabin Site. If you are still driving, this is a good place to park so you get a little warm-up before you start the climb.

The Ride: 0.0 mile – From Holmes Cabin Site (8.5 miles from Packer Lake, continue out the gravel road, which turns into a dirt road. 1.2 miles – The OHV trailhead takes off to the left. (The road to the right is a wild downhill ending in Sierra City!). There is a sign at the Trailhead: *Sierra Buttes Lookout 1 1/4 miles - OHV Road ends 1 mile.* Now the climb begins! If it hasn't rained in a while the road surface will be quite loose, and you may find yourself pushing more than you think you should. The OHV road runs straight up the ridge, then pushes out into an open brushy area with no shade. It appears that this side of the Buttes burned off several years ago and hasn't grown back yet. The view into the North Yuba River Canyon – 3,000 feet below – is sensational! You can see the Pacific Crest Trail winding its way 7 miles down to Sierra City. After the road crosses the Pacific Crest Trail, it turns back into a forested area and continues the climb.

3.2 miles –The OHV road and the trail meet. There is a large sign that reads *No Vehicles Beyond This Point.* If you are here on a busy weekend, this is a good place to leave your bike. But if it isn't crowded, you might want to ride the last half mile to the top. Here the road narrows and has several hairpin turns with magnificent views. 3.7 miles – The road ends, and the stairway to the lookout begins. If it's clear when you visit the Lookout, you can see Mt. Shasta and Mt Lassen far to the north. Closer and down below are Upper and Lower Sardine Lakes, Deer Lake and Upper Salmon Lake. The large lake to the south is Jackson Meadows Reservoir (see Chapter 3). Carefully make your way down the stairs and back to your bike. ***Caution:*** *Be careful on the way down, especially the first three turns! Watch out for hikers!* The Lookout people told us they get over 100 visitors in the tower on busy summer days. Retrace your route back to your car or campsite.

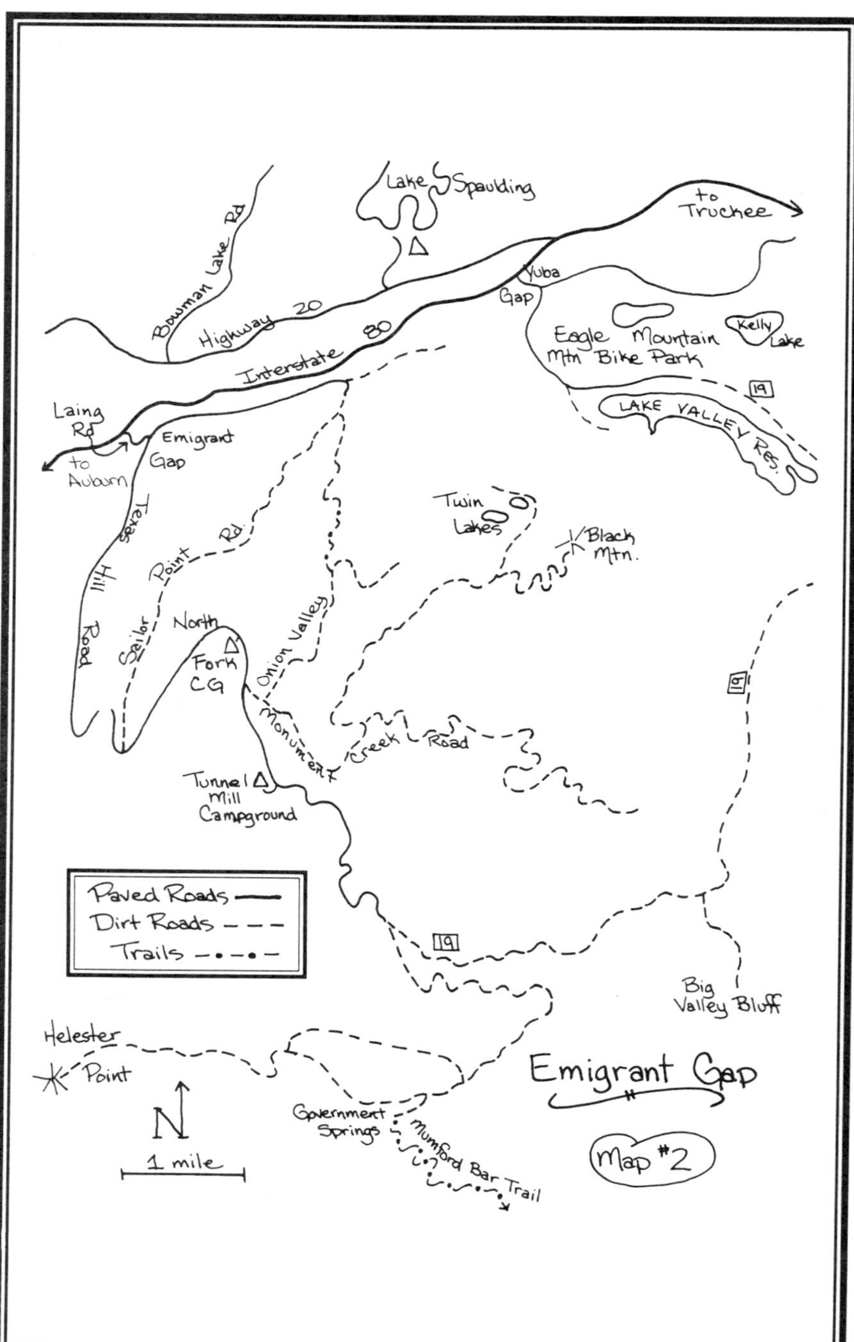

Lake Spaulding
to Truchee
Bowman Lake Rd
Highway 20
Interstate 80
Yuba Gap
Eagle Mountain Mtn Bike Park
Kelly Lake
19
LAKE VALLEY Res.
Laing Rd
to Auburn
Emigrant Gap
Texas Hill Road
Seilor Point Rd
Twin Lakes
Black Mtn.
North Fork CG
Onion Valley
Monument
Creek Road
19
Tunnel Mill Campground
Paved Roads
Dirt Roads
Trails
Big Valley Bluff
Helester Point
Emigrant Gap
N
1 mile
Government Springs
Mumford Bar Trail
Map #2

CHAPTER 2   THE FOOTHILLS
Sailor Point Loop; Sawtooth Ridge Loop; Helester Point;
Onion Valley / Sailor Point; Relief Hill Loop; Martin Ranch

Chapter 2 describes rides in the foothill country of the Sierra Nevada Range within Tahoe National Forest. The elevation in the Emigrant Gap Area ranges from 5,000 to 6,000 feet; in the area of the Malakoff Diggings from 2,000 to 5,000 feet. At these lower elevations the season for mountain bike riding lasts longer than in the higher country. This is the chapter in which you can find rides for late fall and early spring, with certain rides closed only during low elevation snowstorms.

EMIGRANT GAP

Driving up Interstate 80 east of Auburn, the Emigrant Gap area is one of the first sites with easy access to National Forest Lands for mountain biking. To get to this area, take the Laing Road off-ramp, turn right (west) on Emigrant Gap Road. Soon, Emigrant Gap Road ends and become Texas Hill Road. The rides in this section all radiate from Texas Hill Road. Here, you ride through foothill canyons from 4,500 to 6,500 feet, following the many forks of the North Fork American River.
Topo Maps: Blue Canyon, Cisco Grove, Duncan Peak, Westville, 7.5 min., or Emigrant Gap, Duncan Peak, 15 min. All rides start and end from North Fork Campground, T16N, R12E, Section 8.
Campgrounds: USFS Campgrounds North Fork and Tunnel Mill (a group campground) are located on Texas Hill Road. North Fork Campground has a water system.
Seasons: April through mid-November, depending on snow level.
Nearest Services: None at Emigrant Gap; bring all supplies with you. The closest town to the west is Colfax. To the east, Cisco Grove has small stores and gas stations. You can purchase major supplies in Truckee. If you need bike parts, Eagle Mountain Bike Park is located 2 miles east on Interstate 80; follow the signs from Yuba Gap off-ramp.

Ride #1 - Sailor Point Loop
The Sailor Point Loop is part chip seal and part dirt. It can be started right at the Laing Road off-ramp from Interstate 80. If you're looking for a winter ride in the snow, this loop is a good one to try, providing the snow is not too deep.
Level of Difficulty: Intermediate or long beginner. Climbing is done, for the most part, on broken chip seal; the dirt portions are rocky, but not technical.
Mileage: 16 miles.
Elevation: 4,760 ft. to 5,410 ft.
Water: At North Fork Campground and at streams along the ride. Be sure to filter or treat all water you take from mountain streams.

The Ride: 0.0 mile. From North Fork Campground, turn left and ride up Texas Hill Road – part paved, part broken up chip seal – back to Emigrant Gap. 7.0 miles – Continue on the main road east, past the Laing Road off-ramp to Interstate 80, past

Carpenter Flat. When you reach the *Do not enter* sign for another freeway off-ramp at 8.0 miles, stay to the right . 8.2 miles – Turn right when the pavement ends. Continue past a few homes, then up a hill and across a PG&E ditch. Stay right at the next intersection. 10.0 miles – You come to a gate (closed in winter) and the start of Sailor Point Road. This road, a combination of dirt and river rock, goes down the oak and pine forest, climbing its way up onto a ridge. Follow the main road out the ridge; then the downhill begins. Sailor Point Road ends at 13.9 miles. Turn left on Texas Hill Road and continue on downhill back to the campground.

Ride # 2 – Sawtooth Ridge Loop

Level of Difficulty: Intermediate or better. Beginners might want to drive to the top of the ridge at the 3.3 mile point and ride from there, eliminating the steep climb.
Mileage: 18.5 miles. 12 miles if you drive to the top of the ridge.
Elevation: 4,560 ft. to 5,600 feet.
Water: At North Fork Campground and at streams along the ride. Be sure to filter or treat all water you take from mountain streams.

The Ride: 0.0 mile – From North Fork Campground, turn right onto Texas Hill Road. Ride past Onion Valley, the big meadow on your left. 0.5 miles – When the road splits, stay right on Forest Road 19, following the signs to Tunnel Mill Campground and Helester Point. Forest Road 19 goes downhill, following the East Fork of the North Fork of the American River. 1.5 miles – Ride past Tunnel Mill Campground, then begin the climb up to Texas Hill. 3.3 miles – At the top of the ridge, turn right, folowing the signs to Helester Point. Forest Road 19 turn left here. (See Ride #4.) 3.5 miles – A road takes off to the right and circles around Texas Hill for another ride option. Continue straight ahead. The road winds into Burnett Canyon, crosses the creek then winds back out the other side of the canyon and climbs up onto Sawtooth Ridge. The view gets spectacular as you ride along the edge of Sawtooth Ridge, with a 3,000 feet drop-off to the North Fork of the American River. The Foresthill Divide Area, Chapter 7, is located on the ridge to the south.

7.2 miles – The road splits and either way will take you to Helester Point. The best route is to go left, following the sign to the Mumford Bar Trail, marked *19/16/9*. 7.8 miles – A road to the left with a gate across it leads to Government Springs and Mumford Bar Trail. (Mumford Bar Trail is only for really adventurous riders. Those who are strong enough can actually ride down into the canyon 3,000 feet below to the American River, then climb back up the other side to Foresthill Divide. *Don't try the trail alone. Be sure to look at a topo map first.)* Continue straight ahead. 9.1 miles – When Road 19/16/9 ends, you must make a decision. Ride #3 continues on to the left. To finish Ride #2, turn right and follow the signs to North Fork Campground and Interstate 80. 11.2 miles – Back at the intersection with the road to Mumford Bar, continue straight ahead and follow your tracks back to the campground.

Ride #3 – Helester Point

Level of Difficulty: Intermediate or better. This ride is a longer version of Ride #2 and involves an additional 5 miles with a lot of short ups and downs.
Mileage: 24 miles out and back.
Elevation: 4,760 ft. to 6,410 ft.

The Ride: 0.0 mile – From North Fork Campground, follow the description for Ride #2 for the first 9.1 miles. Then turn left (west), following the signs to Helester Point. From here the road is easy to follow; just stay on the main road. This road goes down and up several times, following the Sawtooth Ridge line out, then descends to an old lookout point, 2.6 miles farther on, ending with a magnificent view into the canyon below. When you have finished enjoying the view, follow your tracks back to the last intersection. 14.3 miles – Road 19/16/9 takes off to the right. Go straight ahead at this point. When you reach the intersection for the road to Mumford Bar, continue straight ahead and follow your tracks back to the campground.

Ride #4 – Big Valley Bluff

Level of Difficulty: Intermediate. The ride out is almost all up, so the return trip is fun and easy. Beginners may want to try this one by driving to the end of the pavement at the 3.3 mile point. From there it's a moderate 6.5 mile ride.
Elevation: 4,760 ft. to 6,409 ft.
Mileage: 13 miles total.

The Ride: 0.0 mile – From North Fork Campground follow Ride #2 for the first 3.3 miles. At 3.3 miles continue on out Forest Road 19, following the signs to Big Valley Bluff. Stay on the main road, passing several roads which lead off right and left. Continue to climb up on the ridge. 6.5 miles – Turn right at the sign to Big Valley Bluff. Forest Road 19 continues straight ahead. The road climbs 100 feet higher, then as you get out onto Big Valley Bluff you descend to a view point looking down into the steep North Fork of the American River Canyon, more than 3,000 feet below. When you have enjoyed the view, follow your tracks, climbing back up the bluff. From this point the ride is nearly all downhill to the campground!

Ride #5 – Onion Valley / Sailor Point Loop

Level of Difficulty: Intermediate or strong beginner; for those who enjoy a bit of adventure trying to find old abandoned roads to ride. The ride can be done in both directions.
Elevation: 4,560 ft. to 5,410 ft.
Mileage: 9 miles.

The Ride: 0.0 mile – From North Fork Campground, turn right on Texas Hill Road. 0.5 miles – At Onion Valley, turn left at the sign to Monument Creek. 0.6 miles – Turn left again and ride along the southeast side of Onion Valley which is one large meadow after another. 1.6 miles – Just before the top of the hill, look off to your left for an old road that is almost overgrown with brush. Ride out the old, narrow road that crosses a creek and climbs up through a rocky wash. (You may

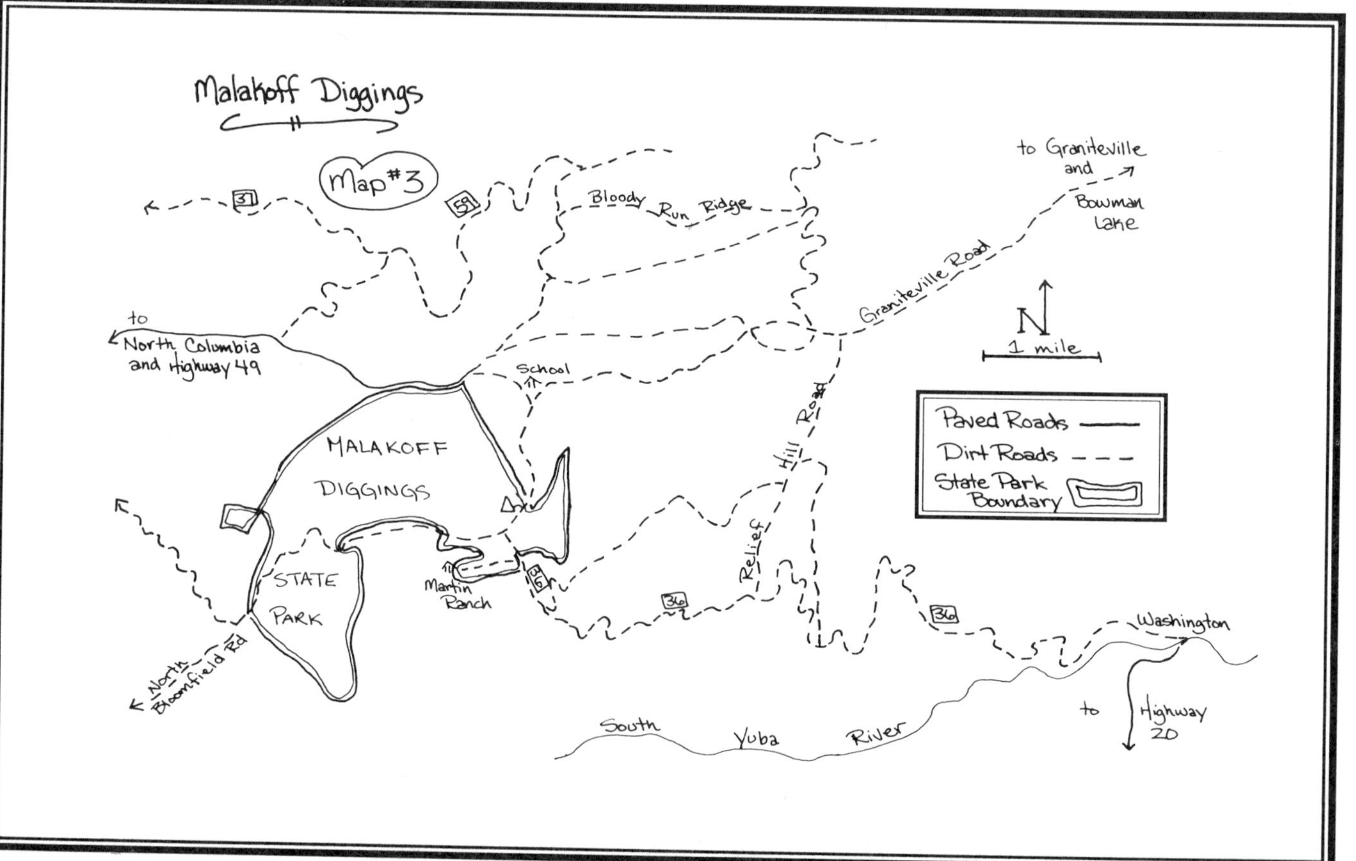

Malakoff Diggings
Map #3
to Graniteville and Bowman Lake
Bloody Run Ridge
Graniteville Road
to North Columbia and Highway 49
School
N
1 mile
Paved Roads
Dirt Roads
State Park Boundary
MALAKOFF DIGGINGS
STATE PARK
Martin Ranch
Relief Hill Road
North Bloomfield Rd
South Yuba River
Washington
to Highway 20

have to walk a short section here.) Once you're on top, the road gets better and better and widens out. Stay on the main road which takes you past some homes. 3.1 miles – When the road ends at a large opening, turn left and you should see a green Forest Service Gate signed *Sailor Point Road.* Ride out Sailor Point Road which climbs at first, then goes downhill. 7.1 miles – Turn left on Texas Hill Road and enjoy the downhill back to the campground.

MALAKOFF DIGGINGS

Located on the western edge of Tahoe National Forest is Malakoff Diggings State Historic Park. Every trip to the Northern Gold Country should include a visit to Malakoff Diggings to see the effect of large scale hydraulic mining done throughout the foothills of the Sierra Nevada. Within the Park is the site of the largest hydraulic gold mine in the world (operated 1866-1884). Although the mining tore away nearly half a mountain, the destruction resulted in the creation of cliff walls similar to the sandstone spires and natural formations found in Utah. You can view this site by mountain bike from the roads. But to get a closer look you have to walk because all the hiking trails within the Park are closed to mountain bikes. The State Park is on the edge of the National Forest, so finding a place to ride is not a problem if you stay here.

To get to the Park, take Interstate 80 to Auburn; go north on Highway 49 through Grass Valley and Nevada City. Twelve miles north of Nevada City, turn right on Tyler Foote Crossing Road and continue to the park.

Topo Maps: Pike, Washington, North Bloomfield, Alleghany, 7.5 min . Alleghany, 15 min. All rides start from the campground T18N, R10E, Section 31.
Campgrounds: A small campground is located at the State Park, with a small lake nearby for swimming and fishing.
Water: Within the campground and at several locations throughout the park.
Seasons: Malakoff Diggings State Park is open year-round. Elevation levels range from 2,000 feet to over 4,000 feet, so you can try winter riding here unless there is a low-elevation snowstorm.
Nearest Services: Small stores are located along Highway 49, but major supplies, gas and bike parts are available in Nevada City.

Ride #6 – Relief Hill Loop
The Relief Hill Loop ride takes you out of the State Park into the National Forest with an option of riding farther out to the historic town of Washington where you can see several old restored buildings.
Level of Difficulty: Strong beginner to intermediate, with a gradual but steady climb in the beginning and a steep fast downhill. All of the road surfaces are good dirt with a minimal amount of rocks. (The optional ride to Washington is difficult.)
Mileage: 13 miles; 29 miles if you detour out to the town of Washington and then complete the loop.
Elevation: 3,300 ft. to 4,600 ft. If you do the optional ride out to Washington, the road goes down into the canyon to 2,600 ft. to the South Yuba River.

The Ride: 0.0. mile – From the campground turn left on the main road that climbs back up to the ridge. 0.8 mile – When the road splits at the grammar school, stay right and ride past the school. The road through here is gravel, dirt, with oiled sections. 4.0 miles – Continue straight ahead at the four-way intersection, staying on the gravel road. 5.8 miles – Turn right on the dirt road signed *Snowtent Rd./Relief Hill.* Your uphill is over and now it is time to start back down into the canyon. 6.9 miles – A road takes off to the left. Continue on down the hill following the signs to Relief Hill. 8.4 miles – The road to the left goes to the town of Washington, 8 miles farther, another historic town you might want to visit by bike. To finish the loop, stay to the right following the signs to North Bloomfield. Soon you will pass by some old cabins and new homes. Continue on. 11.2 miles – When the road ends, turn right. The road to the left goes to the town of Relief. 12 miles – You are back in the Park in the historic town of North Bloomfield. Turn right, ride past the museum, and stay on this road back to the campground

Ride #7 – Martin Ranch

Level of Difficulty: Easy. This short, easy ride takes you through the Park, then on to a fire road to the old Martin Ranch. Suitable for children.
Mileage: 3 miles out and back.
Elevation: 3,200 ft. to 3,400 ft.

The Ride: 0.0 mile – From the campground, turn right and ride back down to the old town of North Bloomfield. 0.5 miles – Turn left on Relief Road, also marked Forest Road 36. The hiking trail to Martin Ranch takes off on your left. Bikes are not allowed on the trails so continue a short distance on Relief Road to the fire road. 1.0 miles – Look off to your right and you should see the fire road closed off by a wood pole gate. Go around the gate and ride out the fire road to the Martin Ranch. 1.5 miles – Explore the old Martin Ranch site, then return to the campground by retracing your tracks.

CHAPTER 3   INTERSTATE 80 – BOWMAN LAKE
Shotgun Lake; Island Lake Loop; Glacier Lake; Faucherie Lake; Canyon Creek; Bowman, Weaver and McMurray Lakes; Meadow Lake; Eagle Mountain Bike Park

The Bowman Lake Area is located 40 miles east of Auburn, north of Interstate 80, at elevations between 5,500 and 7,500 feet. The fun about riding here is that there are so many lakes so close together that you can ride to several in one day! This is a wonderful spot to visit if you enjoy canoeing, swimming and fishing in addition to mountain biking. Trails and roads are very well marked. You will be riding in and out of private and public lands, so always remember to respect the private property signs.

There are three ways to get here. One is to drive east on Interstate 80 and take the Highway 20 off-ramp (1 mile east of the Yuba Gap turn-off), following the signs to Nevada City. Go west on Highway 20 for 3.5 miles to Bowman Lake Road (Forest Road 18). Follow the signs along the Bowman Lake Road to the trailhead or campground of your choice. Be aware that most of the side roads are dirt, and the main road turns to dirt just before reaching Bowman Lake, 13 miles out. The road along the north shore of Bowman Lake is quite narrow in spots and definitely more fun on a bike than in a car!

Another approach is to take Highway 49 north to Tyler Foote Crossing Road. Go east past North Columbia and Malakoff Diggings to the town of Graniteville. From Graniteville continue east on a county road following the signs to Bowman Lake. This is the route that the US Forest Service recommends for passenger vehicles and trailers.

To access the northern part of this area, go 17 miles north of Truckee on Highway 89, turn left (west) on Forest Road 07 and drive 16 miles to Jackson Meadow Reservoir. Forest Road 07 is paved all the way to the reservoir but turns to dirt just past the campgrounds.

Camping: There are plenty of undeveloped US Forest Service campgrounds here. They have outhouses, but may not have tables or water systems. No fee is charged at undeveloped campgrounds. The better camping facilities, complete with water and tables, are located at Jackson Meadows Reservoir, Grouse Ridge and Lake Spaulding. There is public land available for primitive camping, but be aware that there is also a great deal of private property that is posted *No Camping, No Trespassing.* Also, in certain parts of this area camping is allowed only within the campgrounds. (Closed areas are marked on the Tahoe National Forest Map.)
Seasons: Late May through October.
Nearest Services: Take everything you need with you (food, ice, gas), since there are no services once you leave Interstate 80 or Highway 89. Nearest bike shops are in Truckee or at Eagle Mountain near Yuba Gap, off Interstate 80.

CARR LAKE TRAILHEAD

To get to Carr Lake, drive 8.5 miles out Forest Road 18 and turn right on Forest Road 17. Follow the signs to Carr and Feely Lakes, 4 miles farther. There is a small primitive campground located along the shore of Carr Lake. Forest Road 17 is dirt, so if you have a new car you may choose to start riding from Forest Road 18, which will lengthen all of the following rides by 8 miles (4 miles each way).

These rides can also be done from the campground at Grouse Ridge. Take the Grouse Ridge Trail northeast out of the campground towards Milk Lake. Follow the directions for the rides below from the trail intersection at the 2.2 mile point.

Topo Maps: English Mountain and Graniteville, 7.5 min., or Emigrant Gap, 15 min. Carr Lake Trailhead is located at T18N, R12E, Section 28.
Water: There are lakes and streams everywhere. Be sure to filter or treat all drinking water.

Ride #1 - Shotgun Lake
Level of Difficulty: Beginner trail riding.This is a short fun ride. Although most of this route is single-track, many trails are wide old jeep roads. Some riders may have to get off and push through very short uphill sections. For a more challenging ride continue past Shotgun Lake, following directions for Ride #2.
Mileage: 10 miles out and back.
Elevation: 6,600 ft. to 7,100 ft.

The Ride: 0.0 mile – From Carr Lake, turn left on the road just before the outhouses in the campground. Ride uphill to Feely Lake. 0.1 mile – You arrive at Feely Lake and the Round Lake Trailhead (12E26) for Island Lake, Milk Lake and Grouse Ridge Campground. Continue on the Round Lake Trail. 1.0 mile – After you pass a pond and a small lake, the trail forks. The left fork is called Crooked Lake Trail, 12E11. (This is the trail you will return on if you choose to do the Island Lake Loop). Stay to the right, ride up over the ridge and you will arrive at Island Lake. 1.5 miles – Stay on the main trail. (The fork that leads to the right goes to Round Lake.) 1.6 miles – Turn right on the main trail. 1.7 miles – Turn left, following the sign to Milk Lake. 2.2 miles – At the top of a small hill you reach another intersection. The trail straight ahead goes to Grouse Ridge Campground. Off to the right is Milk Lake. Take the Grouse Ridge Trail to the left, following the sign to Glacier Lake and Sawmill Lake.

3.0 miles – At another intersection, stay to the left on the Grouse Ridge Trail. (The road to the right goes to Glacier Lake Trail, 13E13.) 4.3 miles – You reach Middle Lake, which is on its way to becoming Middle Meadow. Continue on the main trail. 4.7 miles – You reach a large meadow and a new section of trail that keeps you up on the rocks and out of the wet meadow. 5.0 miles – You arrive at Shotgun Lake, which is also almost a meadow. From here you can continue on 0.8 mile farther to the edge of the canyon. When you are ready, follow your tracks back to Carr Lake.

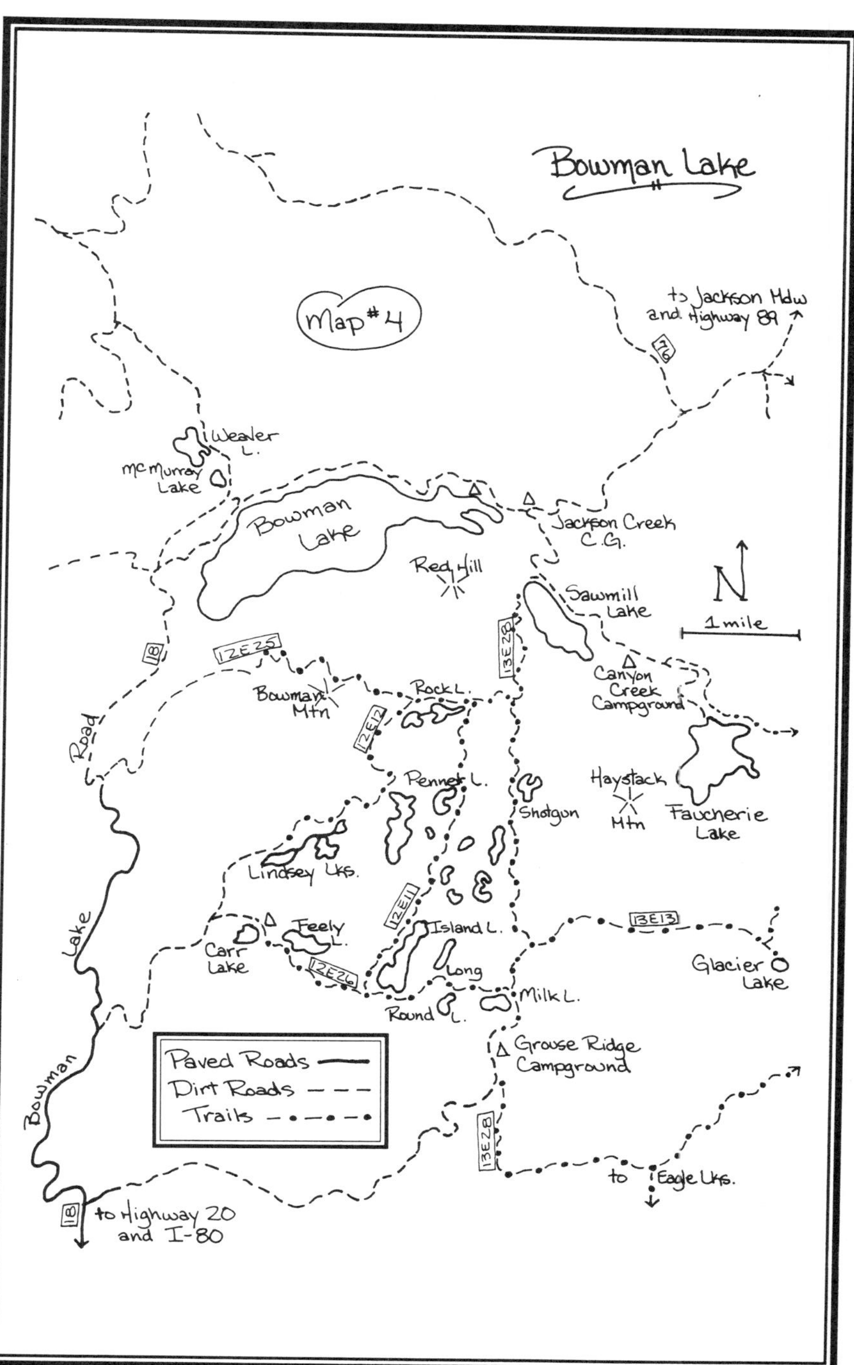

Bowman Lake
Map #4
to Jackson Mdw and Highway 89
7E
Weaver L.
McMurray Lake
Bowman Lake
Red Hill
Jackson Creek C.G.
Sawmill Lake
N
1 mile
18
12E25
13E28
Bowman Mtn
Rock L.
Canyon Creek Campground
12E12
Haystack Mtn
Faucherie Lake
Pennet L.
Shotgun
Road
Lindsey Lks.
12E11
Island L.
13E13
Glacier Lake
Feely L.
Carr Lake
12E26
Long
Milk L.
Round L.
Lake
Grouse Ridge Campground
Bowman
Paved Roads
Dirt Roads
Trails
13E28
to Eagle Lks.
18
to Highway 20 and I-80

Ride #2 - Island Lake Loop

Level of Difficulty: Advanced. Don't be fooled by the low mileage of this ride. It gets rough after you leave Shotgun Lake. *Warning! Do not continue if you think the ride to Shotgun is tough, go back the way you came.* This section of trail is very rocky and very technical, but also very scenic and enjoyable for those in the right frame of mind who don't mind walking occasionally. Great for people who enjoy trials riding or like to work on bike handling skills.
Mileage: 11 miles.
Elevation: 6,600 ft. to 7,100 ft. You will lose and gain 500 feet several times throughout this ride.

The Ride: 0.0 mile – From Carr Lake, follow the directions for Ride #1 to Shotgun Lake. Continue north on the main trail. 5.8 miles – At the edge of the canyon turn left on the trail signed *Bull Pen Trail 12E12, Rock Lake 1 mile.* Straight ahead the Grouse Ridge Trail descends 1 mile to Sawmill Lake. You can ride down to Sawmill Lake for a longer ride, but you will probably have to push your way back up to this intersection. *Warning! On the maps this trail looks like it easily connects to the road on the other side of Sawmill Lake, but if there is a lot of water flowing out of Sawmill Lake the creek crossing is quite dangerous.* You may have to go downstream quite a distance before finding a safe place to cross.

Walk and ride your bike up 380 feet to the top of the ridge. 6.8 miles – At the top, stay left and follow the signs to Penner Lake. (Rock Lake is off to the right. Another option here is to ride out to Lindsey Lake and follow the dirt road back to your car.) After a short downhill, most people will have to walk up some of the next section, which climbs another 400 feet before dropping down to Penner Lake. 7.5 miles – Stay on the trail that follows along the east shore of Penner Lake. *Be careful as you climb and descend through the next rocky sections.* You may want to lower your seat and let some air out of your tires, but don't let too much air out because these sharp rocks could easily puncture a tire. 8.6 miles – You will begin to pass Crooked Lakes off to the left (east). 9.0 miles – Begin the final rocky downhill to Island Lake. The trail continues along the west shore. 9.5 miles – You are back at the intersection of trail 12E26 to Grouse Ridge. Turn right to return to Carr Lake. 10.4 miles – Feely Lake. Continue on to the spillway and back to your car.

Ride #3 - Glacier Lake

Level of Difficulty: Intermediate or better riders that have trail riding experience.
Mileage: 12 miles out and back.
Elevation: 6,600 ft. to 7,600 ft.

The Ride: 0.0 mile – From Carr Lake, follow Ride #1 the first 3 miles. 3.0 miles – Go right on Trail 13E13 following the signs to Glacier Lake. This trail continues on another 3 miles and climbs about 500 feet to the lake. There are places you may have to push your bike. 6.0 miles – Enjoy the lake, which is surrounded by the Black Buttes. When you are ready, follow your tracks or ride back to the intersection and do Ride #2.

JACKSON CREEK CAMPGROUND TRAILHEAD

Jackson Creek Campground is located just east of Bowman Lake. Take Interstate 80 to Highway 20 and turn right on Bowman Lakes Road. Continue on along the north shore of Bowman Lake (the road turns to dirt just before the lake). Jackson Creek Campground is located just past the lake. You can also reach this area from the northeast by taking Highway 89, turning west on Forest Road 07 and continuing to Jackson Meadow Reservoir. After you pass the Jackson Meadow Campground area the road turns to dirt. Continue southwest 3.7 miles to Jackson Creek Campground. If you would rather not drive your car on dirt roads, camp at Jackson Meadows Reservoir and do the rides from there. This will add an additional 8 miles to each of the following routes (4 miles each way).

Topo Maps: English Mountain 7.5 min., or Emigrant Gap 15 min. Rides start from T18N, R12E, Section 2.
Camping: USFS campgrounds are located at Jackson Meadows Reservoir, Bowman Lake, Canyon Creek and also at Jackson Creek, where the rides begin.
Water: These campgrounds do not have water systems, with the exception of those at Jackson Meadows Reservoir. Water is not a problem in summer because the lakes are all controlled by utility companies, and the flow is usually good year-round. Be sure to filter or treat all water from mountain streams.

Ride #4 - Faucherie Lake
Level of Difficulty: Easy beginner ride, scenic and enjoyable for all riders. This is a fun ride on good dirt road with rocky sections. Watch your speed on the way back down – the rough sections may catch you by surprise.
Elevation : Gradual 500-foot gain, 5,600 ft. to 6,123 ft.
Mileage: 8 miles out and back.

The Ride: 0.0 mile – From Jackson Creek Campground, ride south on Faucherie Road. 1.2 miles – Continue straight at the intersection. The road to the right goes to Sawmill Lake, which you could go explore now or on your way back. (Ride out to the spillway, and if you hit it at a time when there is water spilling over the top you will be treated to a series of spectacular water falls!) 2.0 miles – A spur road to the left goes over to a waterfall on Canyon Creek. If you can hear the falls, then it is probably worth riding over to take a look. Continue straight ahead on the main road. 2.5 miles – Continue on past Canyon Creek Campground, another nice place to camp. 3.8 miles – You arrive at Faucherie Lake, clear blue and surrounded by barren, granite peaks. A quiet place to spend the day fishing, swimming and picnicking, this also looks like a nice lake for canoeing. Be sure to ride across the dam to see if water is going over the spillway. Across the spillway you should be able to see a rocky road, which is the road you take to Canyon Creek (Ride #5). When you are through exploring and swimming, follow your tracks back to your car.

Ride #5 - Canyon Creek

Level of Difficulty: Intermediate or better. Even though this is a very low mileage trip, it is not for beginners. It is good for those who enjoy mountain biking as an adventure, and don't mind pushing their bikes a bit to get to those hidden spots that very few people visit. It has fun trials riding sections, and Upper Canyon Creek also looks like a great place to try your luck at fishing.
Elevation: 5,600 ft. to 6,400 ft.
Mileage: 9 miles out and back.

The Ride: 0.0 mile – From Jackson Creek Campground, follow Ride #4 for the first 2.5 miles. 2.5 miles – Turn left on the road just across from Canyon Creek Campground. Stay to the right. This is the back way to the Faucherie Lake spillway. The road is short but fun if you enjoy rocky, trials-type riding. 3.5 miles – When you reach the spillway, there may be a lot of water flowing out of the lake and the road might be under water for a short distance. Walk along the left shore and you should be able to get around the flooded section and get back to the road. 3.7 miles – You ride along the shores of Faucherie Lake, heading back to the inlet of Canyon Creek.

As you leave the lake and begin to follow the creek, the road turns into more of a trail and becomes even rockier in spots. Some may choose to continue on foot; others will find this section a challenge. 4.4 miles – The trail reaches a large bend in the creek with cascading rapids and waterfalls. If you continue from here you will have to portage your bike around a cliff to get to Weil Lake about 0.5 mile farther upstream. (I would recommend walking from this point.) When you have finished exploring, follow your tracks back to camp.

Ride #6 - Bowman, Weaver and McMurray Lakes

Level of Difficulty: Basically a beginner ride with one good climb. Beginners may choose to ride to the end of Bowman Lake and back instead.
Elevation: 5,623 ft. to 5,850 ft.
Mileage: Weaver Lake and back, 9 miles. Bowman Lake spillway and back, 6 miles.

The Ride: 0.0 mile – From Jackson Creek Campground ride west on the Bowman Lakes Road. 0.7 mile – You reach the upper end of Bowman Lake and the Bowman Lake Campground. For the next 2+ miles, the road follows the shoreline of Bowman Lake. Watch for traffic – the road is quite narrow! 2.7 miles – Turn right on the dirt road that immediately starts to climb. There should be a sign here that reads *McMurray Lake 1 mile, Weaver Lake 2 miles.* This road climbs steeply to the top of a ridge and McMurray Lake. From here the road goes gradually downhill. 4.5 miles – Weaver Lake, elevation 5,688 ft. Prepare for a fun downhill back to Bowman Lake and follow your tracks to the campground.

Option from Weaver Lake: The road continues past Weaver Lake and from the map it looks like you could make a long loop around Pinole Ridge on Forest Road 41, then turn right on Forest Road 76, which takes you back to the Bowman LakesRoad and Jackson Creek Campground. If you choose this route you will be riding in and out of private land. The total mileage for the loop is about 19 miles. Carry a topo map and a National Forest Map.

Ride #7 - Meadow Lake
Level of Difficulty: Intermediate. You will gain 2,000 feet in elevation; however, the road surface is all dirt and not too technical.
Elevation: 5,623 ft. to 7,600 ft.
Mileage: 19.5 miles out and back.
Topo Maps: 7.5 min. English Mountain and Webber Peak, or 15 min. Emigrant Gap and Donner Pass.

The Ride: 0.0 mile – From Jackson Creek Campground go east following the signs to Jackson Meadows Reservoir. The road climbs about 600 feet in the next two miles, travelling mainly through private land. Off to your right you will see English Mountain Ranch, a large meadow with English Mountain in the background. 2.8 miles – Turn right on road 19N11, following the signs to Catfish Lake and Meadow Lake. 3.8 miles – The main road continues past Catfish Lake, which is surrounded by private land. From here it goes downhill about a mile before it begins to climb, gradually at first, then rather steeply in spots back up to over 7,600 feet. 8.8 miles – The climbing is over and you get to enjoy a downhill to Meadow Lake. 9.7 miles – At the intersection turn left to ride along the shore of Meadow Lake. When you are ready to return, follow your tracks. There will be a couple of uphills, but most of the work will be over and the ride back is primarily a downhill run.

EAGLE MOUNTAIN BIKE PARK

Location: On Interstate 80, 38 miles east of Auburn (74 miles east of Sacramento), take the Yuba Gap off-ramp. Turn right and follow the signs about 1 mile farther to Eagle Mountain. Park in the parking lot and go into the lodge to purchase a trail pass.
Campgrounds: The people at Eagle Mountain recommend the campground at Lake Spaulding, located just north of Interstate 80. There are several others located nearby on both sides of the freeway.
Seasons: Eagle Mountain Bike Park is open from late May to October 15.
Nearest Services: Eagle Mountain has a repair shop, and the people there should be able to help you with anything you need for your bike. They also have a good supply of cycling accessories – shorts, shirts, sunglasses, sunscreen, etc. – and a snack bar to take care of your pre- and post-ride food needs. Gas stations and grocery stores are located in Cisco Grove east on Interstate 80.
Details: Call (916) 389-2254 for more information, an events calendar, and for current trail-fee information. The people at Eagle Mountain also lead around-the-park-bike tours, bike handling skills classes, white water raft trips and rock climbing excursions.

Eagle Mountain is a cross-country ski center in the winter that has decided to use its trail system for a mountain bike park in the summer. The bike park is located on

1,100 acres of private land between 5,800 ft. and 6,140 ft. in elevation. Eagle Mountain advertises 120 km. of maintained mountain bike trails.

Eagle Mountain and other winter recreation areas are experimenting with the idea of promoting summer recreation to develop into year-round resorts. Hopefully, we will see this idea catching on at other ski areas. The nice thing about this is that you you can find a place to ride without having to spend too much time searching. Also, it is a great place to go if you have a group with a variety of riding skill levels. The trails and the trail map are clearly labeled according to the degree of difficulty, so beginners can ride the easy loops while the better riders try the more advanced trails. Afterwards you can meet at the lodge for lunch or snacks.

In addition to marked trails, Eagle Mountain has a Trials Area adjacent to the parking lot. Rental bikes – including trials bikes-are available at the lodge. This is a great place to work on your bike handling skills. The park also sponsors a wide variety of summer races and other events, such as Family Day and Full Moon Bike Tours.

CHAPTER 4   INTERSTATE 80 – CISCO GROVE
Eagle Lakes / Fordyce Bridge; Spaulding Lake; Signal Peak Hill Climb; Fordyce OHV Trail to Meadow Lake; Cisco Grove to Lake Sterling or Fordyce Lake; Glacier Lakes Basin Loop; Mossy Pond Loop

INDIAN SPRINGS TRAILHEAD

The rides in this chapter are located along Interstate 80, 45 miles east of Auburn at 5,400 to 7,400 feet near the town of Cisco Grove. Along this section, Interstate 80 travels through a canyon following the South Fork of the Yuba River. Campgrounds are located close to the river so you can bike all day then return to your campsite in the afternoon to swim and fish.

The choice of rides in this area include dirt logging roads, single track trails through the granite plateau of the Lakes Basin Area, and the challenging hill climb up to Signal Peak.

Take the Eagle Lakes turn-off about 2 miles west of Cisco Grove. Go northwest about a half mile to Indian Springs Campground. Find a campsite here, or continue on to the trailhead. To get to the trailhead, turn right on the dirt road that takes off just past Indian Springs Campground. After 0.2 mile, you arrive at the trailhead and parking area, which has a bulletin board and restrooms. If there is a map posted, be sure to stop and take a look. There is private land scattered throughout this area, and if there is heavy logging traffic a warning will be posted here.

Topo Maps: Cisco Grove 7.5 min., or Emigrant Gap 15 min. All rides start from T17N, R12E, Section 24.
Campgrounds: US Forest Service campgrounds are located at Indian Springs and Big Bend, and there is a PG&E campground at Lake Spaulding. All of these are nice campgrounds with access to the South Fork of the Yuba River or the shore of Lake Spaulding. Unfortunately they are also near Interstate 80. The noise settles down at night, but this freeway is busy all the time.
Seasons: Mid-June through October.
Nearest Services: Grocery stores and gas stations are located 2 miles east on Interstate 80 in Cisco Grove. A US Forest Service Ranger Station and information center is located in Big Bend, just east of Cisco Grove. Nearest bike shops would be Eagle Mountain to the west, Truckee to the east.

Ride #1 - Eagle Lakes / Fordyce Bridge
Level of Difficulty: Short, fun and challenging intermediate level ride. It's great for those who like to ride the rocks, or want to learn how to ride them. Eagle Lakes vary in size; most of them partially covered with lilies. If you enjoy swimming, ride on to Fordyce Creek where you will find clear, cold water.
Mileage: 6 miles out and back to Eagle Lakes. Fordyce Bridge is 8 miles out and back.

Elevation: 5,400 ft. to 5,500 ft. This ride is nearly flat if you look on a topo map! But in truth you will gain and lose 100 feet in elevation many times over.
Water: Treated water is available from the campground at Indian Springs. If you need water out on the trail, take it from Fordyce Creek rather than from Eagle Lakes. Be sure to filter or treat all water.

The Ride: 0.0 mile – Ride out the Eagle Lakes jeep road which follows along the power line a short distance and then descends to the west. 0.9 mile – Turn right at the intersection following the sign to Eagle Lakes and Grouse Ridge Trail. (The road to the left goes into private land at Pierce Meadows.) 2.0 miles – The road turns into a rocky, washed-out area where jeeps have developed some detours around the worst spots. If you take the detours this whole section is rideable. 2.4 miles – Stay left on the main road, following the sign to Eagle Lakes and Grouse Ridge. (The road to the right goes to Fordyce OHV and Meadow Lake.) At 2.6 miles, stay right following the OHV arrow, then take the next road to the left about 0.1 mile farther. (If you go right here, the road takes you directly to one of the Eagle Lakes, but the trail ends there and you will have to bushwhack your way around the west shore to get back to the road).

3.0 miles – The road leads you between several of the Eagle Lakes. There are side trails taking off all along this next stretch if you would like to take a closer look. 3.3 miles – The road ends at a turn-around. Look north towards the rocks for the trail that leads to Fordyce Bridge. You will have to portage your bike a bit through the next section, so some people may choose to turn around here. 3.7 miles – The bridge over Fordyce Creek. There are nice spots to picnic and swim both upstream and downstream from the bridge. If you choose to swim, be careful! The water runs swiftly at different times of the summer. It is controlled by a utility company, and even late in August the creek may be quite full. Take a good look at the size of the bridge; at times this creek must be a major river!

On the far side of the bridge is a sign for Spaulding Trail, Beyers Lake Trail and Grouse Ridge Campground. When you are through exploring, follow your tracks back. *Options:* You could ride out the trail to Lake Spaulding (see Ride #2) or continue on the Beyers Lake Trail. However, the Beyers Lake Trail is not recommended for mountain bikes! On the map it looks quite tempting, but we pushed our bikes up the ridge (gaining over 800 feet) before we gave up, only to find we had to push our bikes on some of the downhill!

Ride #2 - Lake Spaulding
Mileage: 14 miles out and back.
Water: Plenty of water is available on this ride. Be sure to filter or treat all stream water before you drink it.

The Ride: 0.0 miles – From the Indian Springs Trailhead, follow Ride #1 for the first 3.7 miles. 3.7 miles – Ride across the Fordyce Bridge, and turn left following the sign to the Spaulding Trail. 4.0 miles – Go left at the sign that reads *Spaulding Lake Trail 12E40, Spaulding Lake 2 miles, Bowman Lake Road 4 miles.* From here

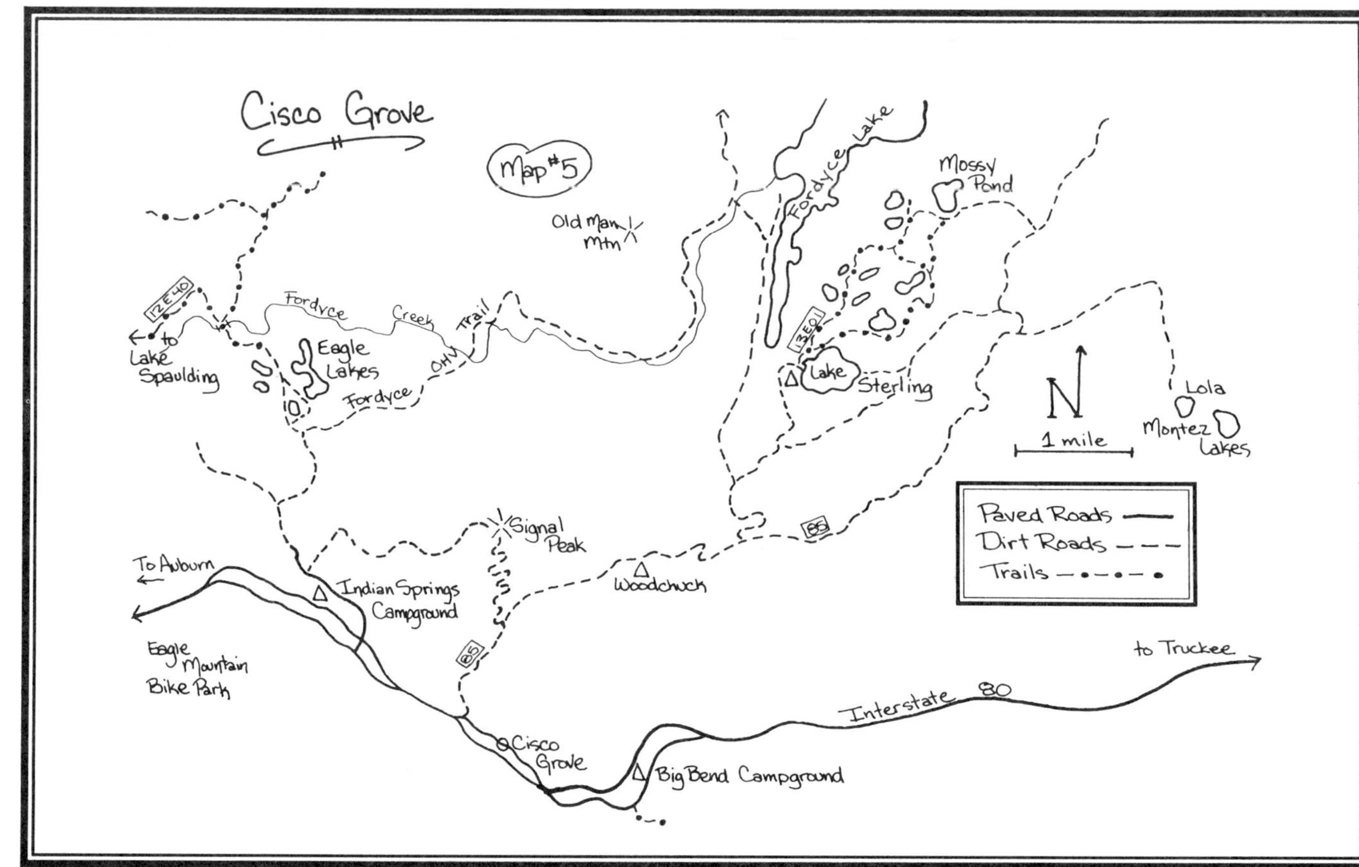

Cisco Grove
Map #5
Old Man Mtn
Fordyce Lake
Mossy Pond
12E40
to Lake Spaulding
Fordyce Creek Trail
Eagle Lakes
OHV
Fordyce
13E01
Lake Sterling
Lola Montez Lakes
N
1 mile
Signal Peak
To Auburn
Indian Springs Campground
Woodchuck
85
85
Eagle Mountain Bike Park
Cisco Grove
Big Bend Campground
Interstate 80
to Truckee
Paved Roads
Dirt Roads
Trails

the trail continues to follow Fordyce Creek downstream. Most of it is rideable, but you will have to carry your bike around a few spots. The peak to the south is Brady Mountain. 5.8 miles – The trail begins to follow along the north shore of Spaulding Lake, leading towards the powerhouse. 7.0 miles – Spend some time enjoying Spaulding Lake and then follow your tracks back. (If you continue on from here the trail becomes a road, and you can ride it to Bowman Lake Road and tie into the rides described in Chapter 3 for the Carr Lake Trailhead.)

Ride #3 - Signal Peak Hill Climb
Level of Difficulty: Advanced ride for those who enjoy the challenge of a rocky hill climb.
Mileage: 8 miles out and back.
Elevation : 5,500 ft. to 7,841 ft.

The Ride: 0.0 mile – The jeep road you are looking for takes off to the right just before the information sign and restroom at the OHV Trailhead. The road is signed: *Signal Peak Jeep Trail.* Another sign says that the road is maintained by a 4-wheel drive club. This ride is easy to follow, just stay on the main 4-wheel drive road that continues to climb to the top of the ridge. The road climbs 1,000 feet quickly within the first 1.5 miles. Then, as it turns north the climb continues, but at a more gradual incline. 3.4 miles – When the road turns east again, prepare yourself for the final 800 ft. of climbing to the top. Once on top enjoy the view down into the South Yuba River Canyon, rest and then prepare for a rapid descent down the mountain! Don't forget the rough sections.

Ride #4 - Fordyce OHV Trail to Meadow Lake
Level of Difficulty: Advanced riders who know how to use a map and compass.
Mileage: 20 miles out and back.
Elevation: 5,500 ft. to 7,300 ft.

Warning! *If you want to ride this route, check with the PG&E personnel at Spaulding Reservoir to see if the Fordyce Crossing is advisable.* From what I hear, this trail is rideable and is a good route for mountain bikes as long as you can safely cross Fordyce Creek, approximately 2 miles out. You may have to stop there, even in late summer. The flow of Fordyce Creek is controlled by PG&E, and we were told stories of Toyota pick-ups being washed downstream as they tried to cross the creek in August.

The Ride: 0.0 mile – Start from the Indian Springs Trailhead and follow Ride #1 for the first 2.4 miles. At that point, turn right and follow the Fordyce OHV Trail and the sign that reads: *Meadow Lake 10 miles.*

From here, you are on your own. When we tried this trail during the summer of 1989, there was helicopter logging being done on the section of private land that the jeep trail traverses. The helicopters fly low and are very quick, so at the time it was not safe to ride.

If you decide to try this route, the road climbs 600 feet in the first 1.5 miles, then drops back down to the Fordyce Creek crossing. After Fordyce Creek, the road follows along the creek and gradually climbs over the next 5.5 miles. The last 3 miles are another 1,400 feet uphill to Meadow Lake (elev. 7,287 ft.). This is another out-and-back ride, but there are several options of longer loops if you are looking for a spot to do some bike camping. (See Chapter 3, Ride #6.)

LAKE STERLING / GLACIER BASIN

The rides listed in this section can be done from Big Bend Campground near Cisco Grove, or shorter loops can be ridden directly from Lake Sterling. Lake Sterling (6,887 ft.) is remote, although it is just 6.5 miles northeast of Interstate 80. The winding, mountain road to the lake turns to dirt just as it leaves Cisco Grove. If you have a new car or a car with low clearance, you should start the rides from Cisco Grove or from Big Bend Campground. Lake Sterling lies on the edge of National Forest property within the section of Forest that is still checkerboarded with private land. There is an abundance of logging roads to explore within this area, but please respect the private property signs.

Topo Maps: Cisco Grove, Soda Springs and Webber Peak 7.5 min., or Donner Pass and Emigrant Gap 15 min. Rides start from Cisco Grove T17N, R13E, Section 29, or from Lake Sterling T17N, R13E, Section 10.
Campgrounds: There is a small 6-site campground located on the shore of Lake Sterling – a quiet, remote place to camp! There is also a large Boy Scout Camp nearby, so Lake Sterling may not always be as quiet as it was when we visited. Woodchuck Campground is a small campground situated 3 miles northeast of Interstate 80. It may be a better choice if you find that the Boy Scout Camp is in session! Another campground close to this area is the Big Bend Campground located across the South Fork of the Yuba River behind the US Forest Service Station in Big Bend.
Water: Treated water is available at the Big Bend Campground. Lake Sterling and Woodchuck Campgrounds do not have a water system. All water taken from streams and lakes needs to be boiled, filtered or treated before drinking.
Nearest Services: Food, gas stations and restaurants can be found in Big Bend and Cisco Grove. The closest bike shops are in Truckee (east) and at Eagle Mountain (west).

Ride #5 - Cisco Grove to Lake Sterling or Fordyce Lake
Level of Difficulty: Intermediate. There is quite a bit of climbing to Fordyce Lake, Lake Sterling and Lola Montez. The main road up is fairly smooth, but side roads to each of the lakes are rocky.
Mileage: 15 miles out and back for Fordyce Lake; 13 miles out and back for Lake Sterling; 22 miles out and back for Lola Montez.
Elevation: 5,700 ft. to 7,100 ft. (Fordyce Summit).

The Ride: 0.0 mile – From Cisco Grove, go west on Hampshire Rock Road (the main street in town). 0.2 mile – Just before the road ends at Thousand Trails Park, turn right on Rattlesnake Road (Forest Road 85). It turns to dirt and takes you along the edge of the Thousand Trails Park. The road begins to climb after it passes the park. You will ride up a couple of switchbacks, and then the road heads back into a small, steep box canyon on Rattlesnake Creek. 3.0 miles – Pass Woodchuck Campground and continue on the main road. 3.5 miles – On your right is a 4-H Summer Camp. Continue on the main road, which begins to wind its way up the ridge. 4.6 miles – You come to a junction with a sign: *Lake Sterling 2 miles - Fordyce Lake 3 miles - Lola Montez 6 miles.* (Forest Road 85 continues straight ahead 6 miles to Lola Montez Lake. This is an option for a longer ride.) To go to Lake Sterling or Fordyce Lake turn left. After one more hairpin turn and a little more climbing the road reaches Fordyce Summit (7,089 ft.). 5.3 miles – The road forks. Continue straight ahead to Fordyce Lake (2 miles) or turn right to Lake Sterling. Both options are explained as follows:

Fordyce Lake: Get ready for a rough, wild downhill! The road drops from 7,089 feet at the summit to lake level at 6,402 feet in less than two miles! Fordyce Lake is a large, long reservoir in a deep canyon. You can ride along the southeast edge of the lake until you reach the spillway. This is an out and back ride, so when you are ready climb up out of the canyon to the summit and enjoy the downhill back to Cisco Grove.

Lake Sterling: You climb just a little bit more, to 7,200 feet, before descending to the lake. The campground is at the end of the road. There is also a trail to the left that leads to the spillway. It is rideable, but some may prefer to walk. From here you could continue on to Ride #6 or Ride #7. When you are ready, follow your tracks back to your car.

Ride #6 - Glacier Lakes Basin Loop
This ride is a short loop through a granite area with many small lakes and ponds – and it is entirely on single-track! You can start from Lake Sterling, if you camped there, or from Cisco Grove or Woodchuck Campground following Ride #5.
Level of Difficulty: Intermediate to advanced with sections of technical single-track. Everyone will walk in places.
Elevation: 7,000 ft. to 7,200 ft.
Mileage: 3.5 miles, all trail riding, so allow 2-3 hours to make it enjoyable; 16.5 miles from Cisco Grove.

The Ride: 0.0 mile – From the Lake Sterling Campground look around the west shore for a trail. There are several, and they all lead to the spillway. 0.2 mile – Ride carefully across the spillway. Although it is hard to tell, the trail splits on the other side. Go left up what looks like an old jeep trail with hiking switchbacks. 0.3 mile – You reach a sign: *Glacier Lakes Basin Trail 13E01 - Mossy Pond West - Mossy Pond East.* Go left, heading towards Mossy Pond West. 0.8 mile – The trail goes down a short, steep section to the first pond. After crossing a creek it travels past several other small ponds. Except for a few large log crossings and narrow brush areas, this section is quite rideable. 1.4 miles – The trails meet at another intersection signed *Mossy Pond 2 miles - Lake Sterling 2 miles.* To finish the short loop, go right here, heading back toward Lake Sterling. Follow the trail that winds up and down and around more ponds before descending to Lake Sterling. Continue back to the spillway and campground.

Ride #7 - Mossy Pond Loop

Level of Difficulty: Intermediate riders or adventurous beginners willing to walk a bit. It's not a very difficult ride except for the single-track. For an easier route, ride out and back on the 4-wheel drive road to Mossy Pond. This way you can play at the slabs without having to do the single-track.
Mileage: 9 miles;22 miles starting from Cisco Grove..
Elevation: 6,988 ft. to 7,360 ft. (from Cisco Grove 5,700 ft. to 7,360 ft.).

The Ride: 0.0 mile – Follow Ride #6 for the first 1.4 miles. At the sign, go left to Mossy Pond. 2.2 miles – The trail ends at a 4-wheel drive road. From here you can take a detour to the left to two more ponds (this detour will add 0.3 miles to the total). To finish the loop, turn right. 2.5 miles. – The road goes down a steep, fun downhill. 2.8 miles – You arrive at the largest pond, Mossy Pond East. For a good view down into Fordyce Canyon, walk over to the granite rocks on the north end of the pond. To continue the loop stay on the 4-wheel drive road that leaves the lake and heads east. 3.2 miles – The road turns into a hillside of granite slabs! The main route is well marked by "jeepers," 4-wheel drive traffic and there is plenty of room to play on the rocks.This is a great spot to come and play a while! Practice your bike handling skills on the smooth granite or try hopping around in the rockier sections. When you are through playing, get back on the main trail that climbs to the top of the slabs, then leaves the rocks. Next you will ride past a large meadow.

4.7 miles – Go right at the intersection. (The road to the left has a gate on it and enters private land.) You will ride past another meadow before the road begins a brief climb. 5.7 miles – In an uphill hairpin turn, take the road to the right. (For a longer loop continue straight ahead, then turn right when you reach Forest Road 85). 6.8 miles – Continue straight ahead at this intersection. (A right turn here takes you down a wild downhill to the east end of Lake Sterling. It is fun, but you then have to bushwhack your way around the lake to try to find a trail.) After a little more climbing the road turns and you are treated to a great view of Signal Peak to the east and Old Man Mountain to the northeast. Then the road begins to go downhill to the next intersection. 8.2 miles – Turn right and make the final descent back to Lake Sterling.

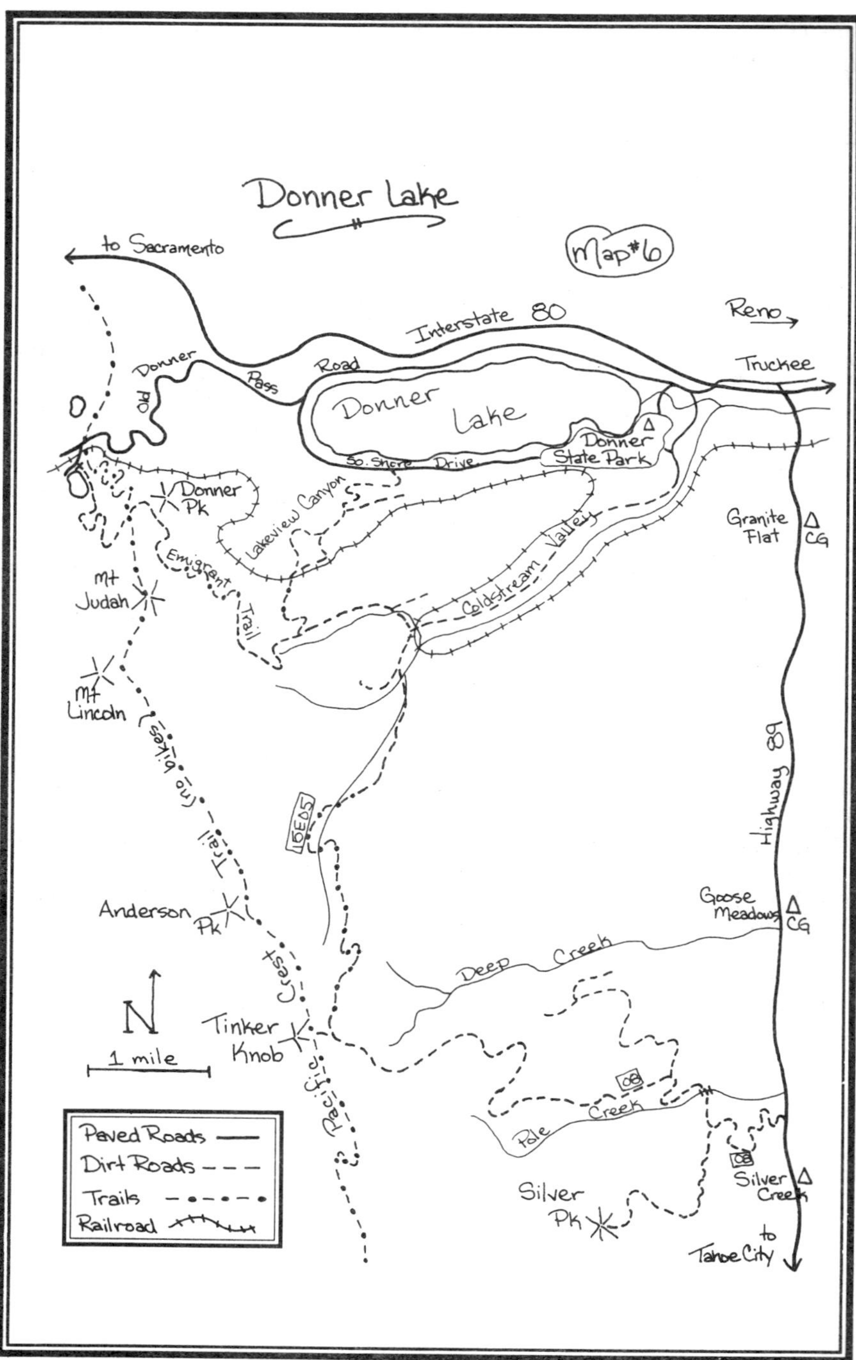

Donner Lake
Map #6
to Sacramento
Reno
Interstate 80
Truckee
Old Donner Pass Road
Donner Lake
So. Shore Drive
Donner State Park
Donner Pk
Lakeview Canyon
Granite Flat
CG
Mt Judah
Emigrant Trail
Coldstream Valley
Mt Lincoln
Pacific Crest Trail (no bikes)
15E05
Highway 89
Anderson Pk
Goose Meadows
CG
Deep Creek
N
1 mile
Tinker Knob
06
Pole Creek
08
Silver Creek
Silver Pk
to Tahoe City
Paved Roads
Dirt Roads
Trails
Railroad

CHAPTER 5   DONNER SUMMIT
Tinkers Knob Loop; Coldstream Valley; Lakeview Canyon Loop; Old Emigrant Trail to Donner Peak

The Donner Summit area is rich in California history. Everywhere you ride, you will be reminded of the early pioneers who travelled through here on their journeys to the west. Monuments are dedicated to the tragic journey of the Donner Party, who tried to cross the Sierra during the winter of 1846-47, and to the amazing tunnel, dug by hand, through the mountains to complete the Central Pacific Railroad. If you enjoy history, be sure to visit the museum at the entrance to Donner Memorial State Park.

This is a wonderful place to visit in summer, but like the rest of the area along Interstate 80, there is a great deal of private land in the vicinity. New gates, *No Trespassing* signs and *No mountain bikes* signs have begun to show up, closing off routes to the public. The Pacific Crest Trail also crosses through this area, and it is closed to mountain bikes. All of the rides in this section go through private land, but they are open to the public and you will find plenty of challenging rides to keep you busy.

Campgrounds: The most popular place to stay here is Donner Memorial State Park, which is open June through September. Make reservations by calling MISTIX at 1-800-444-7275 or the State Park at (916) 587-3841. Three US Forest Service – Silver Creek, Goose Meadows and Granite Flat – are located nearby on Highway 89 between Truckee and Tahoe City. Silver Creek has a water system, but at Goose Meadows and Granite Flat treated water is not available.
Seasons: June through October or until the first major Sierra snowfall. Autumn is a peaceful time to visit the State Park and Museum, and the riding is fantastic after the first fall rain!
Nearest Services: Truckee should have all that you will need: bike shops, grocery stores, restaurants and gas stations.

DONNER LAKE

All of the rides included in this chapter start and end from Donner Memorial State Park located just off Interstate 80 on the shore of Donner Lake.

Ride #1 - Tinkers Knob Loop
Topo Maps: Unfortunately, this ride require four maps! Norden, Truckee, Granite Chief and Tahoe City 7.5 min., or Tahoe, Truckee, Granite Chief and Donner Pass 15 min. Ride starts from Donner State Park, T17N, R16E, Section 18.
Level of Difficulty: For experienced riders in good physical condition. The road to the top gains over 2,000 feet, mostly over very rideable terrain with a couple of short rocky sections that some people may have to walk. The downhill stretch includes over 6 miles of single-track with sections of technical 4-wheel drive roads. The downhill definitely makes the uphill worthwhile!

Mileage: 25 miles.
Elevation: 5,870 ft. to 8,200 ft.
Water: Water is available at several locations along the trail. Be sure to filter or treat all water from mountain streams. Treated water is available at Donner Memorial State Park and Silver Creek Campground.

The Ride: 0.0 mile – From Donner State Park turn right on Donner Pass Road. Ride across Interstate 80 and through a couple of blocks of the town of Truckee. (Fill up your tires to maximum inflation for the first 8 miles of pavement!) 1.6 miles – Turn right on Highway 89, which takes you back under Interstate 80 and then along the Truckee River. 8.3 miles – Just after you pass Big Chief (the name of both the mountain and the building on your left), turn right on a road that takes off beside a white paddle marker with *16* on it. As you start up the first hill, you should see a sign: *Silver Creek 3 miles.* 10.2 miles – Stay on the main road (Forest Road 08) that goes up and then down to a bridge at Silver Creek. Cross the bridge and continue on the main road. 11.7 miles – Turn left at the intersection, following the sign to Upper Pole Creek. ***Warning!*** *The road straight ahead might seem like it heads in the right direction, but you will end up in Deep Creek Canyon instead of Pole Creek Canyon – and do a lot of climbing before the road ends!*

14 miles – Several roads will take off to the left to Upper Pole Creek. Stay on the main road. Soon you will arrive at a meadow, and the scenic part of the ride begins! All around you to the west are gigantic, rocky lava mountains. When you reach an intersection, stay to the right and continue uphill. 14.8 miles – As you go around the ridge, the climbing is over for a short distance and the road drops quickly into Upper Deep Creek Canyon. Tinkers Knob is to the west. Cross the creek and start the final climb to the top. There is one section near the top that most people have to walk. 17.2 miles – Turn right at the top of the ridge on an old jeep road, which is now just a trail. (Off to the left the road continues on as a trail to the top of Tinkers Knob. You may want to ride or hike up it a bit to get a better look at the mountains around you.) Rest if you need to; it is all downhill from this point! When you are ready, start down the trail. It is quite rocky and technical at first.

18.5 miles – The trail crosses the South Fork of Coldstream Creek, and the terrain gets easier as you enter the forest. Continue on. The trail becomes a road. 21 miles – When you reach the railroad tracks, look across and to the left for the main road. Listen for trains, then carefully cross over to the road and continue on through Coldstream Valley. Much of the valley is private land, so respect the *No Trespassing* signs and stay on the main road. When you reach the ponds, stay to the left on the main road. 24.4 miles – You ride through a gate. A short distance farther and to the left is a split rail fence that marks the boundary of Donner Memorial State Park. If you are staying in the Park, take the trail just to the side of the fence near site 101 in Creek Campground. If you are not staying at the Park, continue straight ahead to Donner Pass Road.

Ride #2 - Coldstream Valley

Topo Maps: Norden and Truckee 7.5 min., or Donner Pass and Truckee 15 min. Ride starts at Donner State Park.
Level of Difficulty: Good beginner ride. Most of the terrain is gradual uphill, with one or two short, steep climbs. The farther up Coldstream Canyon you ride, the tougher the riding gets. Most beginners will want to turn around a half-mile or so past the railroad crossing.
Elevation: 5,900 ft. to 6,230 ft.
Mileage: 8 miles out and back to Horseshoe Bend.

The Ride: 0.0 mile – If you are staying at Donner State Park, ride past site 101 in Creek Campground and look for a sign for the overflow parking area. Take the trail to the left that leads to the road going into Coldstream Valley. If you are not staying at the Park, turn south off Donner Pass Road just east of the State Park and follow the signs to Coldstream Valley. 0.2 mile – When you reach the park boundary, stay on the main road that goes through the middle gate (there are three gates), and continue on the paved road. After one steep uphill it levels out and soon turns to dirt. Continue on the main road that passes on the right side of two ponds, then gradually climbs up through the valley. The majority of the valley is private land, so stay on the main road.

3.6 miles – The road brings you to Horseshoe Bend, a spot where the Southern Pacific Railroad makes a sharp turn around the end of the valley. Beginners may want to quit here, but if you would like to ride farther, cross the tracks and continue on. The first mile past the tracks is not too difficult, but if you go much farther you will see why Ride #1 comes down this way instead of up! When you are done exploring, follow your tracks back to the park.

Ride #3 - Lakeview Canyon Loop

Topo Maps: Norden and Truckee 7.5 min., or Donner Pass and Truckee 15 min. Ride starts at Donner State Park.
Level of Difficulty: Easy intermediate ride. There is a steady climb in the beginning, but nothing very technical. It's a fun, short ride with good scenery.
Elevation: 5,960 ft. to 6,840 ft.
Mileage: 11 miles.

The Ride: 0.0 mile – From Donner State Park, ride west through the park along the shore. 1.4 miles – Go around the two gates that mark the western boundary of the Park, and continue riding west on South Shore Drive. 2.7 miles – Turn left on Lakeview Canyon Road. It is hard to find, but if you look carefully you will see a brown Forest Service sign, *Lakeview Canyon,* almost hidden in a patch of overgrown bushes. The road starts off steep, then eases up the rest of the way into the canyon. 3.4 miles – Stay right on the main road and continue climbing. 3.8 miles – Go left and finish the climb up to the railroad tracks. (The right turn also goes to the tracks, but the left is more direct.)

4.2 miles – When you reach the railroad tracks, turn right on the road that follows along the tracks. 4.8 miles – As the railroad tracks begin to curve into Lakeview Canyon, look across the tracks for the power lines. Ride a short distance past the lines and then carefully cross the tracks. Look for a trail that goes up the hill next to the remains of an old building. Follow this trail to the top of the saddle. (It becomes a road on the way up.) 5.0 miles – From the top you can see Squaw Peak and the mountains of Granite Chief Wilderness to the south. 5.4 miles – Turn left at the intersection. You are now riding on the Truckee River Route of Old Emigrant Trail.

6.3 miles – When the road forks, stay right and cross Emigrant Creek. (The creek may be dry by late August.) 6.8 miles – Turn left and ride over to the railroad tracks in Horseshoe Bend. Listen for trains and cross when it is safe. Continue on the main road that goes through Coldstream Valley. (For more details on the next stretch, see Ride #2.) 10.3 miles – After leaving Coldstream Valley, you arrive at a gate that may be open or closed. Go around the gate and continue on. If you are staying at the park, you can enter the campground on the trail next to the split rail fence ahead. If you parked at the entrance, continue riding out the paved road, turn left by the gas stations on Donner Pass Road, and ride back to your car.

Ride #4 - Old Emigrant Trail to Donner Peak
Topo Maps: Norden and Truckee 7.5 min., or Donner Pass and Truckee 15 min. Ride starts at Donner State Park.
Level of Difficulty: Intermediate or better riding skills. Scenic high country ride with a fun downhill on single-track trail and old jeep roads. Some people may have to walk a few short sections of the uphill, but never for very long. A good ride for enjoying fall colors, this route follows a section of the Old Emigrant Trail, which was first marked in 1924.
Mileage : 18.5 miles.
Elevation: 5,940 ft. to 7,840 ft.
Water: Water is available at Donner Memorial State Park. Late in the summer you may not reach water again for 12 miles (Cold Creek). Be sure to filter or treat all water you take from streams.

The Ride: 0.0 mile – From Donner Memorial State Park, follow Ride #3 for the first 5.4 miles. Turn right on Old Emigrant Trail. The road is very rocky at first but smooths out as you begin the climb up Emigrant Canyon. Old Emigrant Trail is very well marked with a variety of older and newer signs. 6.2 miles – When you reach a small round meadow on your right, the road forks in several directions. Take the road that goes straight ahead, just to the left of the meadow. It turns into a trail, and you should still be following the old trail signs. In the next section there may be short uphills that some people will walk, but if the traction is good the uphill is all rideable.

7.6 miles – As you reach a saddle at the base of Mount Judah, the trail again becomes a narrow road. The steep parts of the climb are over, and the road gradually climbs the rest of the way to Donner Peak. 8.9 miles – When Old

Emigrant Trail reaches the saddle behind Donner Peak, look for the monument with a sign: *Emigrant Trail Truckee River Route - Highest Point on the Truckee Route - Elevation 7,850 ft.* From here there is a trail to the top of Donner Peak (elev. 8,019 ft.). Hike up to the top, enjoy the view, and prepare for the fun downhill ahead! When you are rested, follow your tracks back down to the intersection where you first got onto Old Emigrant Trail.

12.4 miles – When you reach the intersection, continue straight ahead on Old Emigrant Trail. 13.4 miles – Stay right and ride across Emigrant Creek. 13.9 miles – When the road ends, turn left and ride up to the railroad tracks. Cross when it is safe and continue on the main road through Coldstream Valley. Stay to the left when you reach the ponds. 17.4 miles – After you leave Coldstream Valley, you arrive at a gate that may be open or closed. Go around the gate and continue on. If you are staying in the park, you can enter the campground on the trail next to the split rail fence ahead. If you parked at the entrance, continue riding out the paved road, turn left by the gas stations on Donner Pass Road, and ride back to your car.

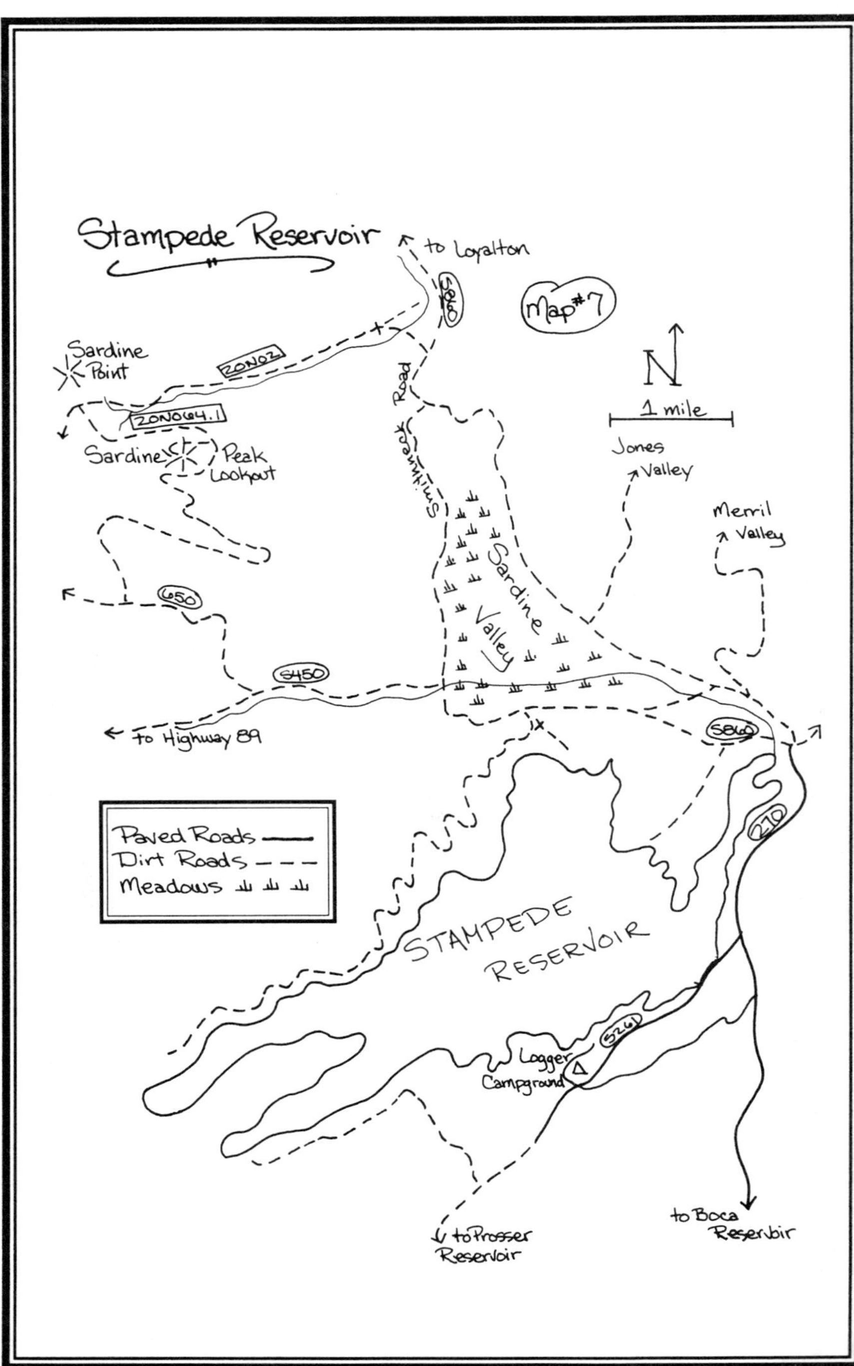

Stampede Reservoir
to Loyalton
Map #7
N
1 mile
Sardine Point
20N02
20N064.1
Sardine
Peak Lookout
Smithneck Road
Sardine Valley
Jones Valley
Merril Valley
650
S450
S860
to Highway 89
270
Paved Roads
Dirt Roads
Meadows
STAMPEDE RESERVOIR
S261
Logger Campground
to Prosser Reservoir
to Boca Reservoir

CHAPTER 6   STAMPEDE / SARDINE PEAK
North Shore; Sardine Peak Lookout Loop; Sardine Valley Loop; Sardine Peak Lookout from Bear Valley; Western Juniper Loop; Bear Valley; Turner Canyon Loop

The Stampede/Sardine Peak area, located to the north of Truckee and east of Highway 89 at the edge of the Tahoe and Toiyabe National Forests, features miles of dirt roads winding through large aspen groves, past giant juniper trees, and through meadows and small valleys following numerous creeks. This is a place for those who enjoy longer rides on good dirt roads with only a few rocky sections. The road system is well signed, which should give most mountain bikers the confidence to explore on their own beyond the rides mentioned here. (All County Roads are marked with road numbers on white paddle markers.)

The best time to visit is in spring, when the meadows are bright green and full of wildflowers. Come in the fall to enjoy the colors of the aspen and cottonwood groves. It can get very warm here in the middle of the summer.

Seasons: May through October or until the first major snowstorm.

STAMPEDE RESERVOIR

Stampede is the largest of three reservoirs located within this area. All three reservoirs – Boca, Prosser and Stampede – have campgrounds along the shore and are good places for boating, fishing and mountain biking. This is a popular summer recreation area, and the campgrounds are usually full on weekends.

Stampede and Prosser Reservoirs were developed right over the Truckee River Route of the Old Emigrant Trail, a route used by pioneers including the Donner Party. If you enjoy history, be sure to visit the Donner Camp Picnic Area near Prosser Reservoir on Highway 89. There is a good historical interpretive trail, and you can easily ride there by mountain bike from any of the campgrounds.

All rides in this section begin and end from Logger Campground at Stampede Reservoir. The rides can also be done from any of the campgrounds within the area by riding to the end of the pavement on County Road 270.

Topo Maps: Boca, Sardine Peak, Dog Valley and Hobart Mills 7.5 min., or Truckee and Loyalton 15 min. All of the rides in this section start from Logger Campground, T19N, R17E Section 30, and they all use the same maps.
Camping: There are USFS campgrounds at all three reservoirs. A small undeveloped campground, Davis Creek, is located at the east end of Stampede Reservoir. Davis Creek does not have a water system, and the creek can be dry by late summer. Camping is allowed only within designated areas.
Nearest Services: The town of Truckee, at the intersection of Highway 89 and Interstate 80, should have everything you need: grocery stores, restaurants and bike shops.

Ride #1 - North Shore
Level of Difficulty: Long beginner ride with very little elevation change. Great for a picnic ride to the far side of the reservoir. Some beginners may choose to turn around before reaching the Little Truckee River, 11 miles out.
Mileage: 24 miles out and back.

The Ride: 0.0 mile – From Logger Campground, turn left on S261. Ride across the dam and continue to County Road 270. 2.0 miles –Turn left on County Road 270. Ride through Hoke Valley to the far end of Stampede Reservoir. 4.0 miles – Turn left at the end of the pavement on Henness Pass Road (County Road S860). A right on Henness Pass Road leads to Dog Valley, another area with many dirt roads to explore by mountain bike. 4.6 miles – Stay right on the main road.

5.6 miles – When you reach Sardine Valley, turn left and stay on the main road (County Road 2860). 6.3 miles – Turn left at a triangular intersection. Ride up a small hill and look for the Forest Service sign that reads: *Day use only beyond this point.* Continue on this road, which takes you back along the north shore of Sardine Reservoir to several nice picnic spots. The upper end of the reservoir, where the Little Truckee River enters, is 5.5 miles farther out (11.8 miles total). Enjoy your picnic by the reservoir, and then follow your tracks back to the campground. (If you are looking for a longer ride, the road continues on from here to Kyburz Flat and loops back into Henness Pass Road.)

Ride #2 - Sardine Peak Lookout Loop
Level of Difficulty: All day distance ride for intermediate or better riders. The roads are all good surface dirt, with only a few rocky sections. The uphill climb of over 2,000 feet is done over several miles and is all rideable.
Mileage: 31 miles.
Elevation: 6,000 ft. to 8,135 ft.
Water: Water is available at Logger Campground and at several creeks along the way. Be sure to filter or treat all water you take from mountain streams.

The Ride: 0.0 mile – Follow Ride #1 for the first 6.3 miles. At that point, continue straight ahead on the main road which heads west and then turns north along the edge of Sardine Valley. 7.3 miles – Turn left on County Road S450 which begins to climb as you enter Davis Canyon. 9.1 miles – Turn right on Lemon Canyon Road (County Road 650). (The road to the left goes to Highway 89, 8 miles away.) 10.5 miles – Turn right at the sign: *Sardine Lookout 4 miles.* The next 4 miles are a steady climb, and you gain 1,500 feet up to the top of the ridge. 14.2 miles – Turn left and continue the last short climb to the lookout tower.

14.5 miles – From the top you can see your starting point, Stampede Reservoir, with Boca Reservoir in the distance and Sardine Valley below. To the southwest are the higher peaks of the Sierra Nevada and Donner Lake. The jagged peaks to the northwest are the Sierra Buttes. When you are through enjoying the view, ride back down to the last intersection. 14.8 miles – Turn left on 20N64.1. (You came up the

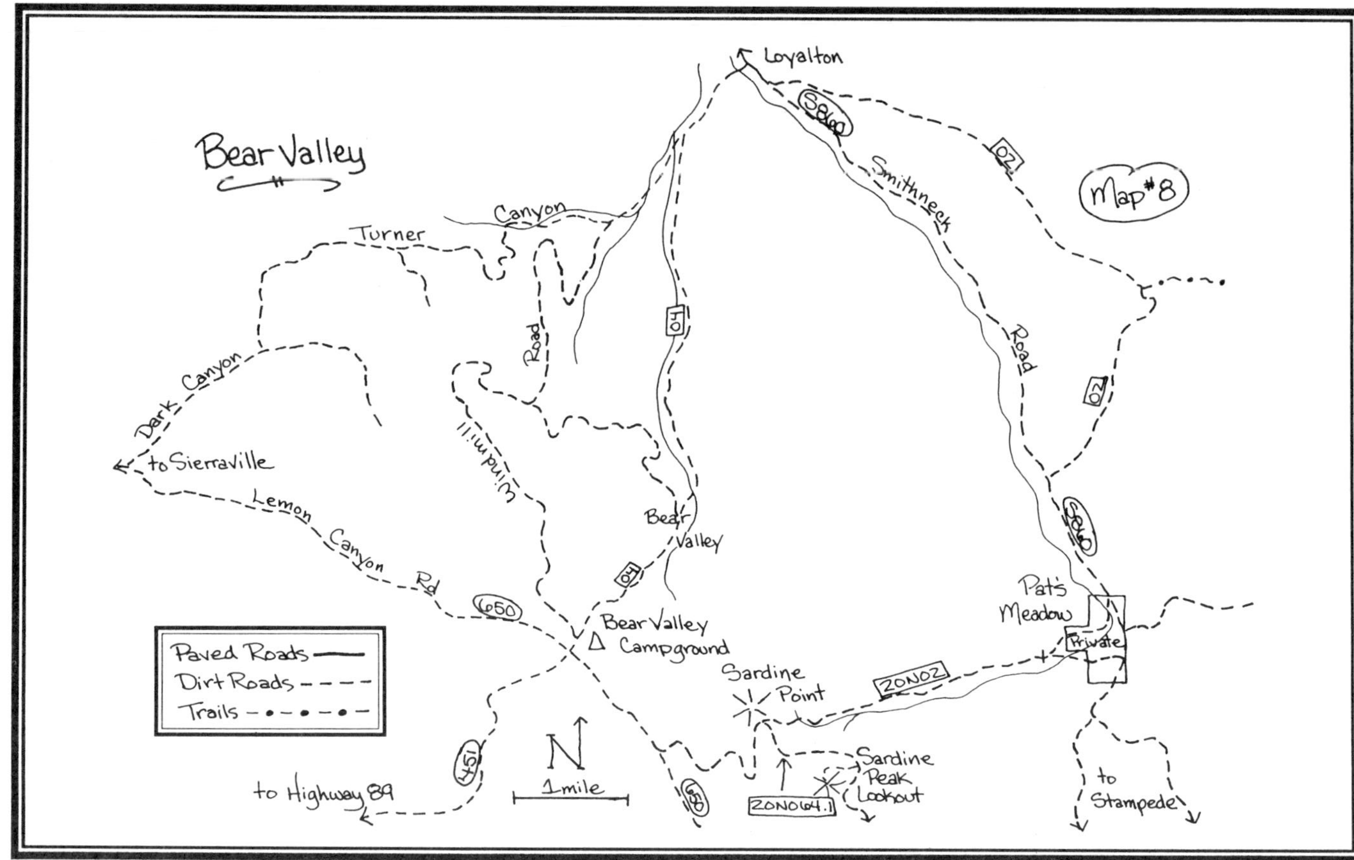

Bear Valley
Map #8
Loyalton
Turner
Canyon
Smithneck
Road
Dark Canyon
01
02
02
to Sierraville
Windmill
Road
Lemon Canyon Rd
Bear
Valley
650
Bear Valley
Campground
07
S840
S840
Pat's
Meadow
Private
Paved Roads
Dirt Roads
Trails
Sardine
Point
20N02
N
451
1 mile
S80
20N064.1
Sardine
Peak
Lookout
to Highway 89
to Stampede

road that is to your right.) 16.4 miles – Turn right on 20N02 and get ready for some downhill fun. 16.9 miles – As you descend, be on the lookout for two huge western juniper trees. The one on the right has a sign stating that it is one of the largest specimens living today. Continue downhill into Trosi Canyon, which if full of aspen and cottonwood trees. This section is spectacular in the fall when all the leaves are yellow, orange and gold! 18.8 miles – Continue past the gate. Be sure to leave it how you found it (open if it was open and closed if it was closed.).

18.9 miles – Stay to the right on the main road. 19.7 miles – When you reach Sardine Valley, turn right on Smithneck Road, following the signs to Stampede Reservoir. 19.9 miles – The road forks as you reach the north end of Sardine Valley. Either fork will take you back to Stampede Reservoir. (These directions continue to the right on Smithneck Road.) 23 miles – County Road S450 takes off to your right, and you are back at the 7.3 mile point. From here, follow your tracks back to the campground.

Ride #3 - Sardine Valley Loop

Level of Difficulty: A long, scenic beginner ride that loops around Sardine Valley.
Mileage: 19 miles.
Elevation: 6,000 ft. to 6,360 ft.
Water: Water is available at Logger Campground and at several creeks along the way. (Be sure to filter or treat the water.) Many of the creeks may be dry late in the summer or fall.

The Ride: 0.0 mile – Follow Ride #2 for the first 7.3 miles. From here Ride #2 turns left, but this ride continues straight ahead to complete the loop around Sardine Valley.

10.4 miles – Turn right at the north end of Sardine Valley. The road goes along the east side of the valley following the power lines. You ride past two roads on the left that go up over the ridge to Jones Valley and Merril Valley. 14.6 miles. Continue on the main road which leaves Sardine Valley and Davis Creek before turning south. When the road ends, turn left on Henness Pass Road. 14.9 miles. Turn right on the paved road and continue back to the campground.

BEAR VALLEY CAMPGROUND

To get to Bear Valley Campground from Truckee, drive 14 miles north on Highway 89 to the intersection of County Road 451 and Forest Road 07. (Forest Road 07 goes to Jackson Meadows Reservoir, which is covered in Chapter 3.) Turn right on County Road 451, Lemon Canyon Road (partially paved), and drive 5.4 miles farther to Bear Valley Campground.

Camping: The smaller Bear Valley Campground is a good place to camp except during the hottest part of summer. (There are no streams or lakes for swimming.)

We were there in late fall. Two campgrounds – Lower LittleTruckee and Upper Little Truckee – are located 11 miles north of Truckee on Highway 89. Both are on the Little Truckee River and both have water systems. The rides in this section can also be done from these two campgrounds. Just follow the directions given for driving to Bear Valley Campground. This will add 14 miles – 7 each way – to your trips.
Nearest Services: There are small stores and gas stations in Sierraville, north on Highway 89. Larger stores, restaurants and bike shops can be found in Truckee.

Ride #4 - Sardine Peak Lookout from Bear Valley

Topo Maps: Sardine Peak 7.5 min., or Loyalton 15 min. All rides in the group begin at Bear Valley Campground, T20N, R16E, Section 30.
Level of Difficulty: Intermediate level hill climb. The road surfaces are all good dirt with only a few short, rocky sections. Beginners in good physical condition should enjoy this ride.
Elevation: 6,594 ft. to 8,135 ft.
Mileage: 13 miles for the loop; 10 miles to Sardine Lookout out and back.

The Ride: 0.0 mile – From Bear Valley Campground, ride southeast out Lemon Canyon Road (County Road 650). It is signed *Sardine Lookout 5 miles, Sardine Valley 7 miles.* 1.6 miles – Turn left and follow the signs to Sardine Lookout. If you ride the loop, you will return to this intersection. From here the road gets steeper as you climb up to Sardine Point. 2.9 mile – When you reach the top of the ridge, turn right on Road 20N64.1 and keep following the signs to Sardine Lookout. After a flat section the road goes up again with one rocky area. Several roads take off from the main road and most of them are clearly marked *Dead End Road.* Just remember to stay on the main road that continues climbing to the Lookout.

4.4 miles – The road straight ahead – County Road 650 – goes to Davis Canyon, and when you complete the loop you will return to this point. Turn right, following the sign to the Lookout. 4.7 miles – From the top of Sardine Peak (elev. 8,135 ft.), you can enjoy a 360° view. Unfortunately the bottom stairs are missing from the lookout tower, but the view is good from the ground, too. To the southeast you can see Sardine Valley, Stampede Reservoir and Boca Reservoir; to the southwest is Donner Lake surrounded by mountains. To the northwest, the jagged peaks you see sticking up from the forest are Sierra Buttes. After you enjoy the view, your choices are to ride back the way you came or follow the directions for the loop.

5.0 miles – To finish the loop ride, turn right and follow the sign that reads: *Davis Canyon 6 miles.* Follow the main road that goes out on the ridge, makes a big switchback, and heads downhill into a small valley. 8.7 miles – When you reach the valley, turn right on County Road 650, Lemon Canyon Road, which winds its way along a creek and takes you through a large meadow. 11.1 miles – You are back to the intersection where the road on the right heads to Sardine Lookout. Continue straight ahead and follow your tracks back to the campground.

Ride #5 - Western Juniper Loop

On the Juniper Loop you will ride past a very large western juniper tree that is signed: *Western Juniper - Juniperus occidentalis*. With a circumference of 30 feet, this specimen represents one of the largest known trees of its species. You will be rapidly descending when you pass the juniper, so be sure to pay attention and look to your right when you get to the downhill on the northeast side of Sardine Peak.

Topo Maps: Sardine Peak and Loyalton 7.5 min., or Loyalton 15 min. The ride begins at Bear Valley Campground, T20N, R16E, Section 30.
Level of Difficulty: Intermediate all-day ride. The entire ride is on good surface dirt roads with two miles of pavement.
Mileage: 20.5 miles (24.5 miles if you ride to the top of Sardine Lookout).
Elevation: 6,594 ft. to 8,135 ft.
Water: Water is available at Bear Valley Campground and at several creeks along the way. (Be sure to filter or treat all water from streams.) There is also water at Loyalton, 17 miles into the ride.

The Ride: 0.0 mile – Follow Ride #4 for the first 2.9 miles to the top of the ridge by Sardine Point. At that point, continue straight ahead on 20N02 instead of turning right and riding to the Lookout. (For a longer ride, detour out to the Lookout for the view and return to this intersection to continue. This adds 4 miles to the loop.) 3.4 miles – As you descend, be sure to look for two large western juniper trees, one on each side of the road. The one on the right has the sign on it. Continue on down into Trosi Canyon, which is full of aspens and cottonwoods. (This is a spectacular ride for seeing fall color!)

5.3 miles – There is a gate across the road. Continue on, making sure to leave the gate how you found it (closed, if closed; open, if open). 5.4 miles – Stay to the right on the main road. (The road to the left goes to the same place, but since it crosses private land, it is best to stay to the right here.) 6.2 miles – When you reach Sardine Valley, turn left on Smithneck Road. (The road to the right goes to Stampede Reservoir.) Continue on past Pat's Meadow. 6.9 miles – The road to Babbitt Lookout (6 miles) takes off to your right, in case you are looking for another ride to try! Continue on the main road that follows Smithneck Creek through more aspen groves and past several good picnic and rest spots. If you look closely, you should see beaver dams all along the creek.

12 miles – The road, now marked County Road S860, turns to pavement. Continue on. Soon you will pass a small memorial picnic spot. This is a nice shady area if you need a break. 13.5 miles – At the edge of the town of Loyalton, turn left on Bear Valley Road. 13.9 miles – The pavement ends and the road gets rough for a short distance. Continue following the signs to Bear Valley Campground. You pass several roads that head west (right), some of which are included in other rides in this chapter. There are several other options for loop rides in this area, and all you need to do is pay attention to the road signs and carry a map.

15.1 miles – Stay to the left as the road begins to climb along Bear Valley Creek. 18.1 miles – The road enters Bear Valley, another large meadow. Continue through the valley and follow the signs back to Bear Valley Campground, another 2.4 miles.

Ride #6 - Bear Valley
Level of Difficulty: Easy; short beginner ride.
Mileage: 5 miles out and back.
Elevation: 6,280 ft. to 6,394 ft.

The Ride: 0.0 mile – From Bear Valley Campground, ride north on Forest Road 04, which rolls along gently climbing and descending small hills to Bear Valley. Ride out to the far end of the valley (2 miles). When you are done exploring, follow your tracks back to the campground.

Ride #7 - Turner Canyon Loop
Topo Maps: Sardine Peak and Sierraville 7.5 min., or Loyalton 15 min. The ride begins at Bear Valley Campground, T20N, R16E, Section 30.
Level of Difficulty: Intermediate level ride for people in good physical condition. The road gains and loses elevation over and over, but none of the climbs require walking. Good spring and fall ride.
Mileage: Turner Canyon Loop is 18 miles; Windmill Road Loop is 13.2 miles.
Elevation: 6,594 ft. to 5,440 ft. to 6,570 ft. to 5,400 ft. to 6,594 ft. Total elevation gain: 2,324 ft.
Water: Water is available at Bear Valley Campground and at several creeks along the ride. Be sure to filter or treat all water taken from mountain streams.

The Ride: 0.0 mile – From Bear Valley Campground, ride north on Forest Road 04. Stay on the main road that goes through Bear Valley and continues into a small canyon following Bear Valley Creek. 5.2 miles – Turn left on the Turner Canyon Road at the sign reading: *Turner Canyon 1 mile - Lemon Canyon 8 miles.* 5.8 miles – Windmill Road takes off to the left. This is an option for a shorter loop back to Bear Valley. (Just stay on Windmill Road and follow the signs 6 miles back to Bear Valley or 8 miles back to the campground.) To finish the Turner Canyon Loop, continue on the main road that begins to climb as it enters Turner Canyon.

8.8 miles – The road levels out on top of Bear Flat, then starts back down the west side into Dark Canyon. 13.2 miles – Turner Canyon ends at Lemon Canyon Road (County Road 650). Turn left. The road begins to climb again as you ride through Lemon Canyon, which is filled with aspens. Stay on the main road that takes you back to Bear Valley Campground (4.5 miles).

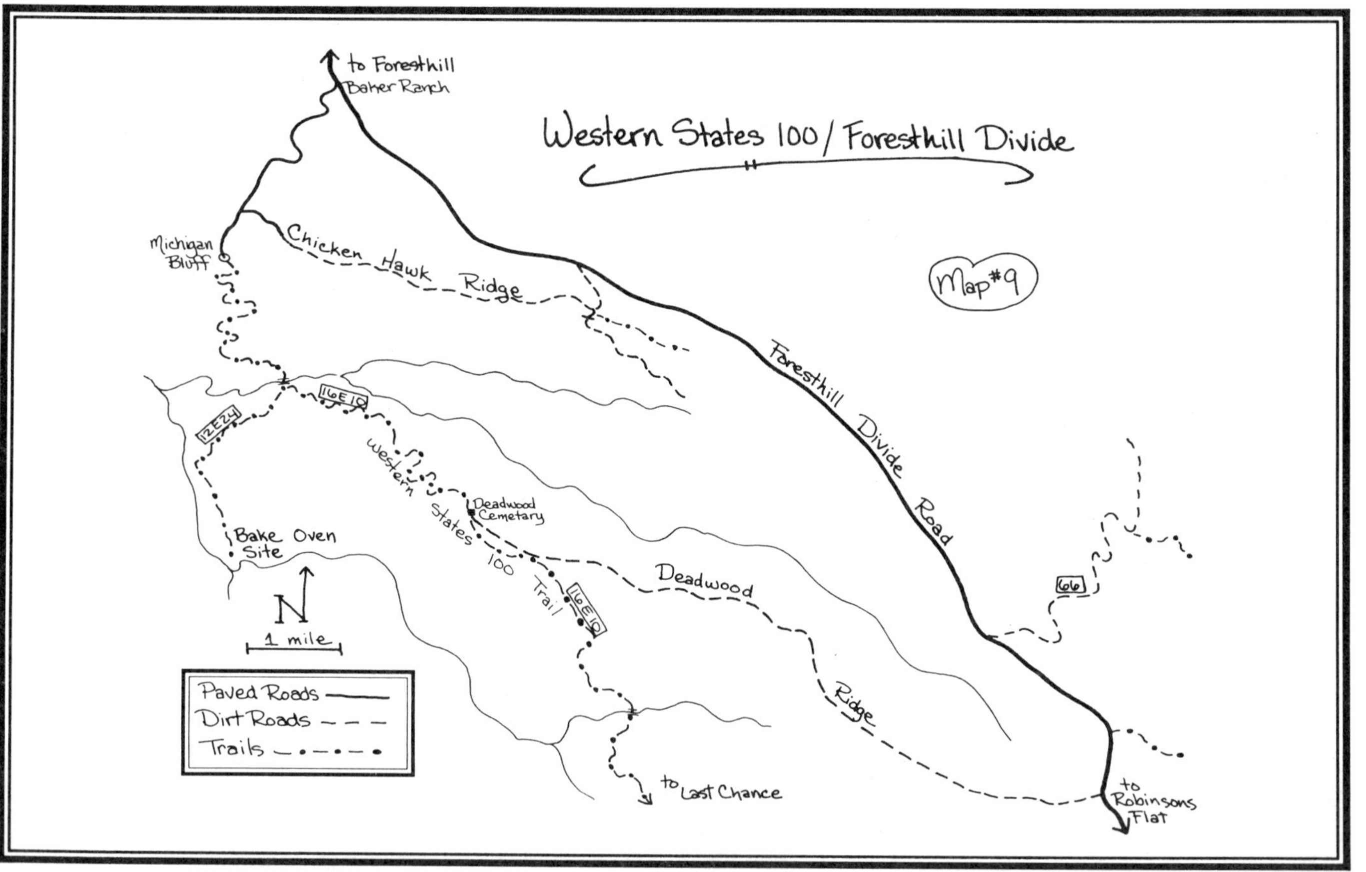

Western States 100 / Foresthill Divide
Map #9
to Foresthill Baker Ranch
Michigan Bluff
Chicken Hawk Ridge
Foresthill Divide Road
16E10
12E24
Western States 100 Trail
Deadwood Cemetary
16E10
Bake Oven Site
Deadwood Ridge
66
to Last Chance
to Robinsons Flat
N
1 mile
Paved Roads
Dirt Roads
Trails

CHAPTER 7   FORESTHILL / FRENCH MEADOWS
El Dorado Canyon Loop; Deadwood to Michigan Bluff; Deadwood Cemetery; Robinsons Flat / Red Star Ridge Loop; Sugar Pine Reservoir Loop; Park Flats OHV Area; Poppy Trail; Granite Chief Bike and Hike; Red Star Ridge Loop

The Foresthill area, located 18 miles east of Auburn, covers a wide variety of terrain from steep, rocky, river canyons lined with oak trees to the high country of Granite Chief Wilderness Area. The Foresthill area, now sparsely populated, was once full of booming gold mining towns. You will be riding on old trails with historical names like "Last Chance," trails that were at one time toll routes. Everywhere you look there are signs of mining that took place here in the 1850s.

These rides all start from different locations along the Foresthill Divide Road. From Sacramento, drive east on Interstate 80 to Auburn. Take the Foresthill exit and continue to Foresthill. At the eastern edge of town where the road forks, stay left on Foresthill Divide Road.

Campgrounds: Several US Forest Service Campgrounds are located along, or a short distance, from the Foresthill Divide Road. Secret House and Robinsons Flats are "undeveloped" campgrounds (no piped in water). Nicer campgrounds can be found at Sugar Pine Reservoir and at French Meadows Reservoir.
Seasons: Mid-May through October. See the individual rides for more details.
Nearest Services: The town of Foresthill should have all that you need in the way of grocery stores, gas stations and a few restaurants. The closest bike shops are back in Auburn.

WESTERN STATES 100

The Western States 100 is an annual ultra-marathon running event which has become one of the best known in the country. To qualify as a finisher you must run the entire 100 miles in under 30 hours. Runners start in Squaw Valley, climb Emigrant Pass (elev. 8,760 ft.), and finish in Auburn (1,300 ft.). This doesn't sound too bad until you look at the specifics of the race where the actual elevation gain is over 17,000 feet and the elevation loss is over 21,000 feet. This is an extremely tough, challenging course. Much of the Western States 100 Trail lies within Tahoe National Forest, and a large portion is open to mountain bikes. The only part of the trail on National Forest land closed to mountain bikes is that which goes through Granite Chief Wilderness Area.

Many of the rides included in this section will take you on the Western States 100 and follow the route for a few miles. Be sure to read the ride descriptions. This is tough, rugged, isolated country and very challenging mountain bike riding. The rest of the trail is marked on the Tahoe National Forest Map, and if you enjoyed these shorter sections you may want to try some others.

Ride #1 - El Dorado Canyon Loop

The El Dorado Canyon Loop follows along the route of the Western States 100 Endurance Race. This is one of the most challenging rides in *Guide 3B*.

To get to the start from Foresthill, drive out Foresthill Divide Road 4.5 miles to Baker Ranch. Turn right on the road to Michigan Bluff. 2.9 miles farther you will reach the gold rush town of Michigan Bluff. Limited parking is available in front of the homes here. To conserve parking space, the locals like you to park straight in rather than parallel.

Level of Difficulty: Advanced riders only! *Do not try this ride alone.* Depending on the time of year, it could be days before anyone else ventures down the trail. Be sure you feel comfortable with the ability of all riders that go with you. If someone gets hurt it will be up to your group to evacuate them or ride out for help. All rescues must be done on foot. Have fun, enjoy the downhill, but ride carefully! Watch out for rattlesnakes in the canyon and poison oak all along the trail section.

Topo Maps: Michigan Bluff and Westville 7.5 min., or Duncan Peak 15 min. Ride starts from Michigan Bluff, T14N, R11E, Section 22.

Mileage: 31 miles.

Elevation: 1,800 ft. to 5,400 ft. The ride starts at 3,500 feet, climbs to 5,400 feet, descends to 1,800 feet, and climbs back to 3,500 feet.

Water: No water is available at the start of the ride, so be sure your bottles are full when you leave Foresthill. The only water on the ride is at the 27-mile point in El Dorado Canyon. Be sure to filter or treat all water taken from mountain streams.

Seasons: Mid-May through October. Spring and fall (after the first rains), are the best times to do this ride. Avoid the middle of the summer when the canyon is very hot and dry.

The Ride: 0.0 mile – From Michigan Bluff ride back up the paved road you drove in on. 0.6 mile – Turn right on Chicken Hawk Road, which starts off as a paved road. Several roads will go left and right; just stay on the main road that goes northeast out the ridge. 1.2 miles – Stay right on Chicken Hawk Road which becomes a dirt road. The road continues to climb back up on the ridge. If you look off in the distance to the right, you will see the Crystal Range of the Sierra Nevada. 5.5 miles – Chicken Hawk Road ends at wide, paved Foresthill Divide Road. Turn right. For the next 10 miles you ride along the paved road. It is steady, but never steep, as you gain 1,200 feet before going slightly downhill to Deadwood Ridge. This part of the ride is scenic and not difficult, but many may prefer to do the shuttle option described in Ride #2 to avoid riding 10 miles of pavement.

15.3 miles – Turn right on Deadwood Road. Take a break in the shade and prepare for the downhill! First the road takes you gradually down Deadwood Ridge, but it gets steeper and your speed increases. 21.6 miles – Continue on Deadwood Road, passing the Western States 100 Trail that goes east to Devils Thumb. 23.3 miles – Go left on the Western States 100 Trail. Deadwood Road heads to the right and ends up at the same place, but the trail is more fun to ride. 24.2 miles – The Western

States 100 Trail and Deadwood Road meet again at the Deadwood Cemetery. This old cemetery from the gold rush days is all that is left of a town. From here the loop continues down the trail to the left. Please read the warning posted on the trail sign! The trail is not well maintained from this point on; it is very steep and narrow, and it is also open to motorcycles, hikers and horseback riders. *Caution: If you are tired do not proceed! Once you ride down into the canyon the only way out is by bicycle or by foot. If someone is injured it will be up to your group to get help or manage the rescue alone.*

The trail – historically known as the "Last Chance Trail" – quickly begins to drop off into El Dorado Canyon. If you try this ride in the fall after the first rain the big leaf maple trees will be yellow and the air will be filled with the strong scent of bay trees that line the trail. This is a fun, technical section, and all your efforts will be concentrated on negotiating the route. Plan to stop occasionally to shake out your hands and enjoy the view! *Watch out for poison oak the entire way down, and rattlesnakes the closer you get to the river!*

27.7 miles – Cross the bridge over El Dorado Canyon. Below the bridge there is a good swimming hole and a nice place to take a break in the shade. If you are out of water be sure to resupply here. *(Filter or treat all water taken from the river.)* Don't be fooled by the map and assume you are almost back to the car – it's a 3,500-foot climb and a thirsty 3.5 miles away. For many this still won't sound too tough, but the trail winds its way out onto south-facing slopes with very little shade.

When you are rested, start up the trail. There is an old jeep road here too, but it is steeper than the trail, so most people prefer to follow the Western States 100 Trail. If you haven't yet gained a new respect for long distance runners, this next section of trail may convince you! The first part of the climb is the steepest, but the worst part is when the trail heads out into the sunny spots on the south-facing slopes. If you start to feel tired, just think a moment about the runners making their way up out of the canyon. This is the 60 mile point in the race and the lead runners get here after running 10 to 11 hours!

Everyone will push in spots on this climb. Just remember it is only 3.5 miles to your car. Once the trail crosses the creek in Poor Mans Canyon, it becomes more rideable. When it merges with the road it's an easy ride the rest of the way back to your car.

Ride #2 - Deadwood to Michigan Bluff

This is a shuttle ride requiring you to leave one car at Michigan Bluff and one at Deadwood Road. (Follow the directions to Michigan Bluff in Ride #1.) To get to the beginning of the ride from Foresthill, drive out Foresthill Divide Road 17 miles to Deadwood Road.

Level of Difficulty: Advanced riders only. Be sure to read all the warnings mentioned in Ride #1. You will eliminate 15 miles of gradual climbing by doing this ride as a shuttle, but this does not reduce the degree of difficulty. You will only be less tired when you reach the tough sections.

Elevation: 5,400 ft. to 1,800 ft.to 3,500 ft.
The Ride: 0.0 mile – Start riding at the beginning of Deadwood Road. Refer to Ride #1 for directions, starting at the 15.3 mile point. The total mileage one way will be 16 miles – 12.5 miles of downhill with 3.5 miles of uphill at the end.

Ride #3 - Deadwood Cemetery

This is a good ride for less experienced riders who got talked into being the shuttle drivers for Ride #1, or for those who are curious about this ride and would like to see what the Western States 100 trail looks like.

Level of Difficulty: Strong beginner to intermediate. The ride follows a good dirt road all the way, with the option of trying a one-mile section of the trail. Just remember this ride is all downhill on the way out so you will be climbing on the return trip to the car.
Mileage: 18 miles out and back.
Elevation: 5,350 ft. to 3,900 ft.
Water: No water is available on this ride.

The Ride: 0.0 mile – From the intersection of Deadwood Road and Foresthill Divide Road (see directions in Ride #2), ride out Deadwood Road. 6.3 miles – Continue straight ahead. (A road takes off to the left and goes to the Devil Thumb Check Point of the Western States Trail.) 8.0 miles – Here you can either stay right on Deadwood Road or go left and try a section of the Western States 100 Trail. 9.0 miles – The trail and the road meet at the Deadwood Cemetery. Rides #1 and #2 continue on the trail to the left. This ride ends here, and you might want to do some exploring in the old cemetery before heading back to your car.

Ride #4 - Robinsons Flat / Red Star Ridge Loop

Topo Maps: Duncan Peak and Royal Gorge 7.5 min. or Duncan Peak and Granite Chief 15 min. Ride starts from T15N, R13E, Section 11.
Level of Difficulty: Advanced. This is an all-day adventure for experienced riders only. It's challenging, with lots of single-track riding. The elevation profile only shows a total gain of about 1,800 feet, but in reality you will be gaining and losing elevation throughout the ride.
Elevation: 6,700 ft. to 7,200 ft. to 5,400 ft. to 6,700 ft.
Water: The Robinsons Flat Campground does not have a water system, but spring water is available. It is best to bring water with you from home. Out on the ride there is no water until you drop into Duncan Canyon 18 miles into the ride.
Seasons: June through October. We attempted to do this ride May 18th after a mild winter, and we were stopped by snow drifts before we even reached Robinsons Flat.

The Ride: 0.0 mile – From the Robinsons Flat Campground, continue out the county road (Foresthill/Soda Springs Road). It rolls along, gaining and losing elevation for a few miles, and then begins to climb back up as you ride around Sunflower Hill. After this it continues to gain and lose elevation once again. 6.5 miles – Turn right on Forest Road 96 at the intersection, following signs to French

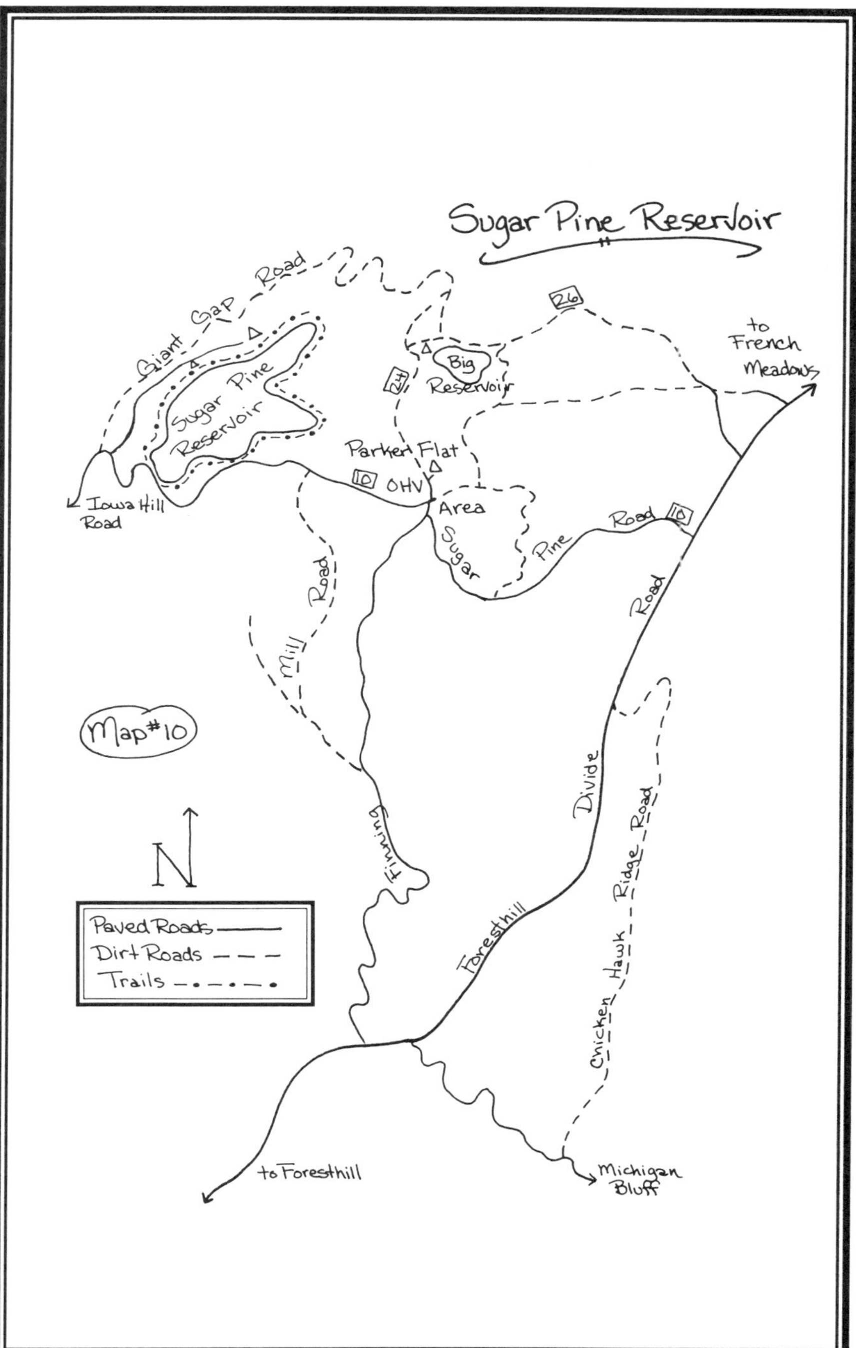

Sugar Pine Reservoir
Giant Gap Road
Sugar Pine Reservoir
Iowa Hill Road
Big Reservoir
27
26
to French Meadows
Parker Flat
OHV
10
Area
Sugar Pine Road
10
Mill Road
Divide Road
Foresthill Divide
Chicken Hawk Ridge Road
Summit
Map #10
N
Paved Roads
Dirt Roads
Trails
to Foresthill
Michigan Bluff

Meadows. (The main county road you have been riding continues all the way to Soda Springs on Interstate 80.) 7.9 miles – The road climbs to the top of the ridge at 7,213 feet. Continue to where a trail crosses the road and you see a sign: *13 miles Robinsons Flat - Tevis Cup Trail - PCT 11 miles.* Go right on Tevis Cup Trail, following the route of the Western States 100. The next 8 miles are all on challenging single-track along Red Star Ridge. Don't think that it will be all downhill! Just like any ridge ride there are many great descents followed by some awesome climbs! You will gain a great respect for the runners who take part in the Western States Run! Most of this section of trail is rideable, but there are a couple of spots that almost everyone will have to push.

15.9 miles – At what appears to be the end of the ridge, turn right on the trail. (Going straight you would encounter a jeep road.) Ride the short, steep downhill and look straight ahead for the wooden signs on a tree: *Western States Trail - Robinsons Flat 6 miles.* Go right here toward Robinsons Flat. The trail gets tougher as it descends into Duncan Canyon. Then it climbs up out of one small canyon and drops down the other side before the final climb begins back up to Robinsons Flat. A series of switchbacks will help you gain the 1,300 feet to get out of Duncan Canyon. 22 miles – The trail ties into Foresthill/Soda Springs Road, which leads back to the campground.

SUGAR PINE RESERVOIR

Sugar Pine Reservoir Recreation Area is located north of Foresthill on the edge of the Tahoe National Forest. To get to the reservoir, drive northeast 9 miles on the Foresthill Divide Road and turn left (north) on Sugar Pine Road (Forest Road 10). Continue 6 miles on the paved road to the reservoir. Off to the right, just before you reach the reservoir, you will see the sign for the Parker Flat OHV Area. There is a small campground here, but the nicer one is located on the shore of the reservoir. Other recreation here includes swimming, fishing and boating.

The following are just two examples of areas to ride in Sugar Pine Recreation Area. This is one of those spots with an endless supply of dirt roads to explore.

Topo Maps: Dutch Flat 7.5 min., or Colfax 15 min. The area is in T15N, R10E, Section 24.
Campgrounds: There is a small "undeveloped" campground at the Parker Flat OHV Area. The better campgrounds are on the north shore of Sugar Pine Reservoir. A group area camp is located on the southeast side of the reservoir and can be reserved by calling the Foresthill Ranger Station, (916) 367-2224.
Water: Water is available at the campgrounds, the picnic area, and at the boat launching area.
Seasons: The majority of the riding in this area is below 4,000 feet and can be ridden almost all year. The roads can sometimes be closed due to low elevation snow. If in doubt, call the Foresthill Ranger Station. The nicest times to visit are in spring and in fall after the first good rain. This area can be hot and dusty in the middle of the summer.

Nearest Services: Foresthill has grocery stores, gas stations and a few restaurants. The nearest bike shops are in Auburn.

Ride #5 - Sugar Pine Reservoir Loop

The path around Sugar Pine Reservoir is one of the first places that I have encountered a sign showing that the trail is designated for bicycle use. It was a pleasant surprise after a day's drive to find the trail and not have to worry if it was OK to ride it!

Please ride conservatively, especially on the paved sections near the campgrounds, since this area is also designated for wheelchair use. If you have any friends confined to a wheelchair, this is a nice spot to take them to enjoy the National Forest.

Level of Difficulty: Beginner. This is an easy, fun, well-maintained trail suitable for riders of all abilities, including children. It's very short, with only one set of switchbacks where the trail is washed out.
Mileage: 5 miles.

The Ride: 0.0 mile – From the campground, ride towards the lake and find the paved trail. Ride southwest towards the dam, and soon the trail will turn to dirt. 0.8 mile – The trail has washed out and you will have to dismount and push your bike back up to the trail. 1.0 mile – You arrive at the dam and a small gate across the trail. It may not look like it at first, but the gate will swing open if you push on it. Ride across the dam and back out to the trail. Continuing around the lake shore, you pass the boat ramp and cross a bridge over Forbes Creek. Then you reach a small log bridge crossing Shirttail Creek that you may have to walk across. 4.2 mile – After crossing the bridge, continue the loop back to the campground.

Ride #6 - Parker Flats OHV Area

Parker Flats OHV Area is located just 0.5 mile east of Sugar Pine Reservoir. There are over 30 miles of signed motorcycle and ATV trails to ride. All the trails are well marked and signed according to degree of difficulty. The easier trails are all rideable by mountain bike; the more difficult ones are fun, but you have to walk some of the steeper sections. You can ride your bike from the campgrounds at Sugar Pine Reservoir to this area and spend the day exploring the trails.

Warning: We visited in the fall on a week day after the first big rain, and no one was there at all. But we have been told that this OHV Area is heavily used on weekends. The Sugar Pine Area is great for riding in spring and fall, but not on a summer weekend!

FRENCH MEADOWS

French Meadows Recreation Area is located 40 miles east of Foresthill. This is a long way from anywhere, but once you arrive the riding is endless. It's a good place for a mountain bike retreat with a group. Other recreation includes boating, swimming and fishing. We saw one fisherman catch a 16" German Brown trout from the Middle Fork of the American River, which flows into French Meadows Reservoir. This area is on the western side of Granite Chief Wilderness Area, and it gets very little use. You can ride to the Wilderness boundary, park your bike, and then enjoy an easy hike into Picayune Valley, which has rocks with Indian petroglyphs. Much of the land lies within a State Game Refuge, so firearms are not allowed. This makes it a great place to try if you are worried about riding during hunting season.

Topo Maps: Bunker Hill, Royal Gorge and Granite Chief 7.5 min., or Granite Chief 15 min. Rides start from T15N, R14E, Section 16.

Campgrounds: Camping is allowed only within designated campgrounds. French Meadows Campground and Lewis Campground – both on the shores of French Meadows Reservoir – are what I consider "full service" facilities with tables, toilets and piped water. Usually these campgrounds are full only on the three big summer weekends: Memorial Day, Fourth of July and Labor Day. Another nice campground is Ahart, located one mile upstream from the reservoir on the Middle Fork of the American River. Ahart has only 12 sites, and during the week we were the only people staying there. Water must be filtered from the stream. Several group camps are available by reservation only; call Foresthill Ranger Station at (619) 367-2224.

Nearest Services: Fill your gas tank when you leave Georgetown or Foresthill. There are no services available, so take all the food, beverages and ice you think you will need. Prepare to be completely self-sufficient, since the nearest bike shops are in Placerville or Auburn.

Ride #7 - Poppy Trail

Level of Difficulty: Intermediate skill level. You should know how to move your bike around rocks, or you will have to walk through the creek drainages.
Mileage: 6 miles out and back.
Elevation: 5,200 to 5,400 ft.

The Poppy Trail – otherwise known as the McGuire Trail – is located on the north shore of French Meadows Reservoir. Either drive or ride your bike along the north shore, following signs to McGuire Picnic Area.

The Ride: 0.0 mile – From the McGuire Picnic Area Entrance, turn right into the picnic area and continue toward the restroom. 0.2 mile – Turn right at the sign which reads: *Trail to Western States Trail - 3 miles to dam - 1 mile to Poppy Campground.* Follow the road to the trailhead. The McGuire Trail is a 3-mile route that leads along the shore to the spillway. 1.2 miles – You reach Poppy Campground, a small area for boaters, bikers and hikers. This is a fun stretch of single-track that doesn't seem to get much use, especially past Poppy Campground. Watch out for hikers and be careful crossing the creek drainages. 2.9 miles – When you reach the spillway, turn around and ride the same trail back.

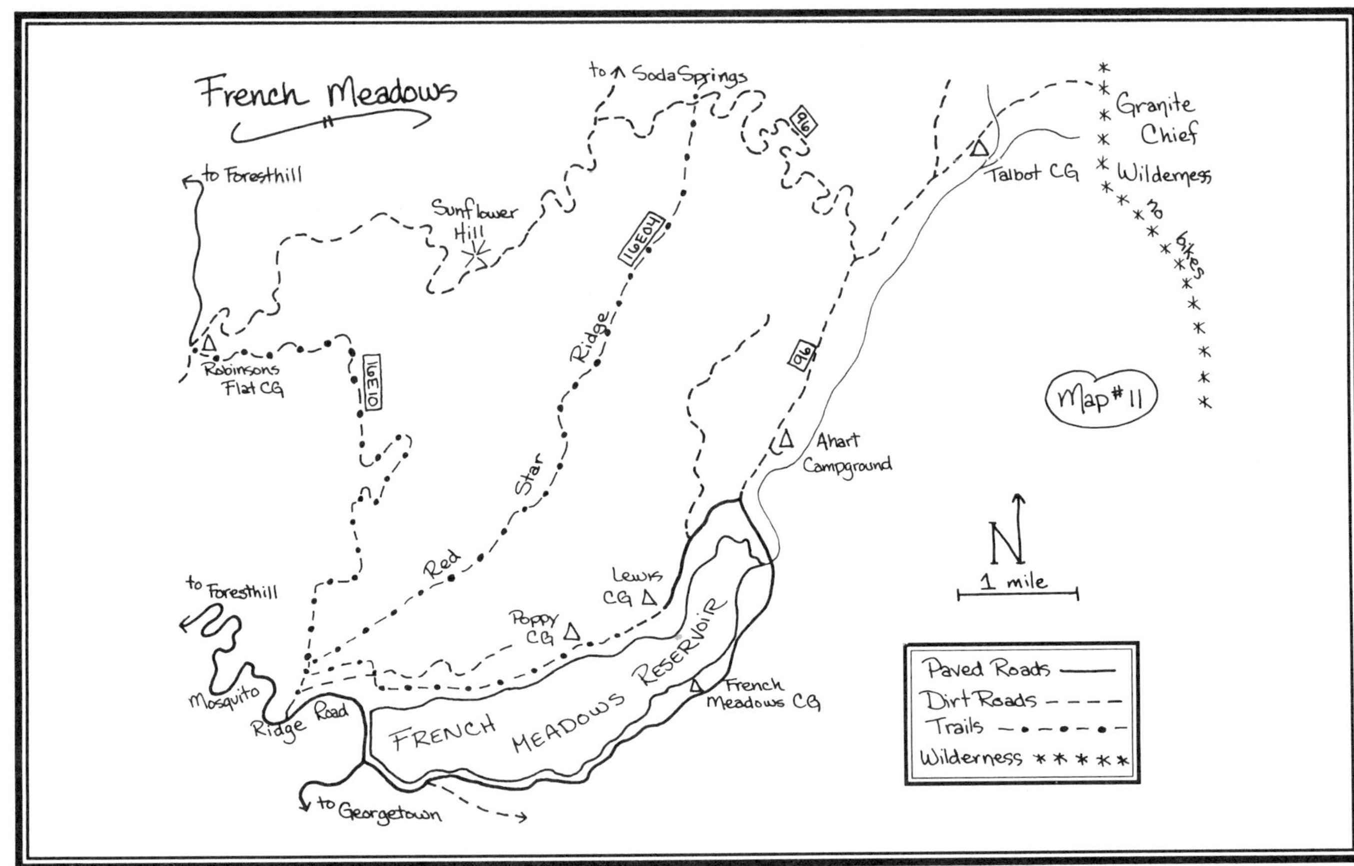

French Meadows
to Soda Springs
96
Granite Chief Wilderness
to bikes
Talbot CG
to Foresthill
Sunflower Hill
16E04
Robinsons Flat CG
19E01
Ridge
96
Map #11
Ahart Campground
Red
Star
to Foresthill
Lewis CG
Poppy CG
N
1 mile
FRENCH MEADOWS RESERVOIR
French Meadows CG
Mosquito Ridge Road
to Georgetown
Paved Roads
Dirt Roads
Trails
Wilderness

Ride #8 - Granite Chief Bike and Hike

Level of Difficulty: Easy. Out and back to the Wilderness Boundary is suitable for children. The addition of the hike to Picayune Valley would be too much for small children, but for others it makes a fun, all-day adventure. Pack a lunch if you decide to add the hike to your bike trip!

Mileage: 10 miles out and back from Talbot Campground. Bike and Hike to Picayune Valley – 19 miles total.

Elevation: 5,300 ft. to 5,800 ft.

The Ride: 0.0 mile – Starting from Ahart Campground, go east on Forest Road 96 and follow the Middle Fork of the American River. 2.0 miles – Continue straight on 16E10. (Road 96 goes uphill and to the left.) There is a sign for Foresthill Divide, Soda Springs and Foresthill. 3.0 miles – Continue straight ahead. The road to the right goes to Dobbas Cow Camp (private land). 3.5 miles – Go right, following the sign for Talbot Campground and Granite Chief Wilderness. 4.0 miles – You arrive at Talbot Campground and are faced with a Vehicle Control Gate at the creek. No motor vehicles are allowed beyond this point. Go around the gate and across the stream; then continue on the main road. 5.0 miles – You arrive at the Granite Chief Wilderness boundary *(No Bikes Allowed!)*. Here you can leave your bikes and hike into the Wilderness Area. An easy day hike of 4.5 miles will bring you to Picayune Valley, a narrow valley surrounded by rock cliffs. Look closely and you may find petroglyphs on the rock walls. This is also supposed to be a great area for fishing. When you are through exploring, hike back to your bikes and ride back to the campground.

Ride #9 - Red Star Ridge Loop

Level of Difficulty: Advanced riders will enjoy the challenge of this ride. With nearly 2,000 feet of climbing, it is not a ride for beginners! The trail section follows the route of the Western States 100 Race and is very technical.

Mileage: 22 miles.

Elevation: 5,330 ft. to 7,180 ft.

Water: Carry all that you think you will need. Red Star Ridge can be hot and dry. There is no water until you return to French Meadows Reservoir, 18 miles into the ride. Be sure to filter or treat all the water you take from lakes or streams.

The Ride: 0.0 mile – Starting from Ahart Campground, go east on Forest Road 96. 2.0 miles – Stay left on Road 96, following the sign marked *Foresthill Divide - Soda Springs - Foresthill*. Stay on the main road that winds in and out continually as it climbs up to the top of the ridge. (You will pass several forest roads that look worth exploring for future rides!) 5.6 miles – As you climb, look for a K-Tag (yellow sign) on a tree on the right that tells you your location is T15 North, R14 East, on the line between Sections 3 and 4. Just past the tag you will be treated to another outstanding view into Picayune Valley in Granite Chief Wilderness Area. 7.0 miles – You reach the top (7,180 ft.) after 1,850 feet of climbing. Enjoy the view of the volcanic rocks to your left (west). From the top, go left on Tevis Cup Trail, following the route of the Western States 100. The next 8 miles are all on challenging single-track along Red Star Ridge. Don't think that it will be all downhill! Just like any ridge ride there are many great descents followed by some awesome climbs! You will gain a great respect for the runners who take part in the Western States Run! Most of this section of trail is rideable, but there are a couple of spots that almost everyone will have to push.

15 miles – At what appears to be the end of the ridge, turn right on the trail. Ride the short steep downhill and look straight ahead for wooden signs on a tree: *Western States Trail - Robinsons Flat 6 miles*. For a longer stretch of single-track, you could go right here (see Ride #4), but stay left to return to French Meadows. 15.3 miles – You reach another intersection with signs for the Western States Trail, Tevis Cup, Robinsons Flat, Poppy Campground, and a parking area. Now it is time for a decision. If you are tired, or tired of single-track trail, go straight ahead to the parking area and turn left on the paved road. This will take you back to French Meadows Reservoir and your campground. If you would like a bit more adventure, go east (to the right as you face the Western States sign) and follow the signs to Poppy Campground. Taking this route, the trail connects with a road after 0.2 mile. Go left on the road for a short distance and then turn right on the trail marked *McGuire Trail - Poppy Campground 2 miles*. This short trail also ends on a road. Go left again and then right at the next intersection. Then follow the road until it ends.

Due to some logging you have to do a bit of hunting to find the McGuire Trail. Just remember to head downhill towards the lake the easiest way possible, and you will intersect the trail that follows closely along the lake shore. Be careful in the many creek drainages and watch out for hikers. This fun section is not too difficult, but it can be rough if you are exhausted. If you are tired, it's best to take the paved road option and save this trail for another day. 17.9 miles – Poppy Campground. 18.9 miles – The McGuire Trail ends on an old road. Go right and continue to McGuire Picnic Area. 19.2 miles – Go left when you reach the restrooms. There is a sign here that reads: *Trail to Western States - 3 miles to dam - 1 mile to Poppy Campground.* 19.7 miles – When you reach the main campground road turn right. 20.5 miles – When you reach Forest Road 96, turn left to return to Ahart Campground. Turn right if you are camped at French Meadows.

Ward Creek

Ward Creek
to Truckee
Paved Roads
Dirt Roads
Trail
Wilderness Boundary
Map # 12
Alpine Meadows Dr.
Truckee River
Highway 89
to Kings Beach
28
Tahoe City
Area
Granlibakken Ski Area
Alpine
Scott Peak
Meadows Ski Area
Paige Meadows
Ward Peak
William Kent C.G.
Granite Chief Wilderness
Ward Creek
no bikes
Stanford Rock
Twin Peaks
Blackwood Canyon
LAKE TAHOE
OHV Staging Area
N
1 mile
Barker Peak
to Barker Pass
Highway 89
to South Lake Tahoe

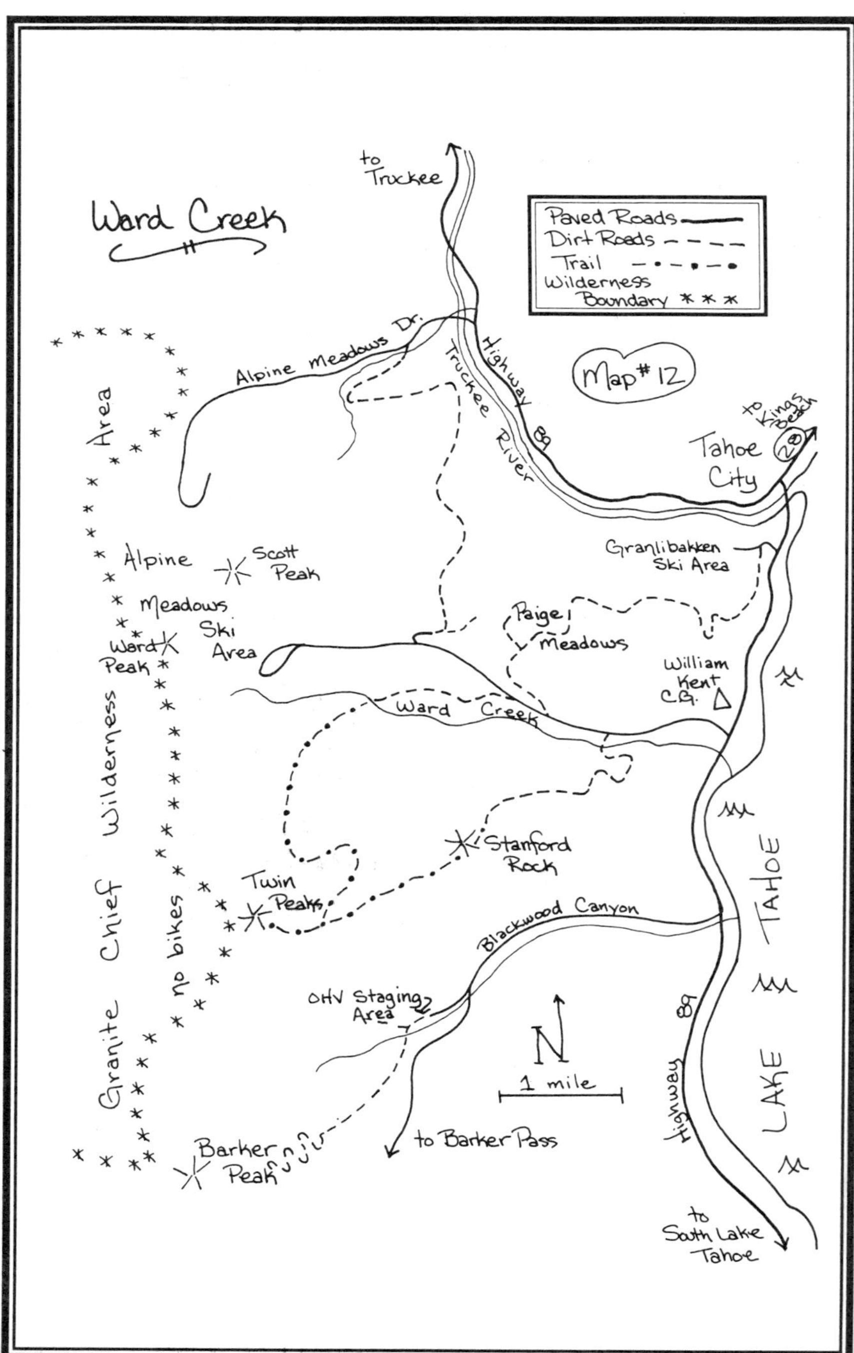

CHAPTER 8   NORTHWEST SHORE LAKE TAHOE
The 21-Mile Spin!; Paige Meadows Loop; Ward Creek; Twin Peaks Bike and Hike; Ellis Peak Loop; Miller Lake Loop; Barker Pass Loop

The majority of rides in this chapter involve exhilarating climbs to mountains with views of Lake Tahoe and the peaks in Desolation Valley and Granite Chief Wilderness Areas.The rides start along the northwest shore of Lake Tahoe between Tahoma and Tahoe City, either from a campground or from a major road that is easy to find. If you are staying somewhere along the northwest shore you can ride the bike trail that runs along Highway 89 to get to the starting points

Nearest Services: Small stores, gas stations and restaurants are located all along this stretch of Highway 89. If you can't find what you need, there are more stores in Tahoe City. Several bike shops are located between Homewood and Tahoe City. If you need more than a tube or a water bottle, look for a shop that does more than just rent bicycles. Some shops have mechanics available to help you with your questions and repairs.
Campgrounds: William Kent, a 95-unit US Forest Service campground, is located in the center of this area, with several other campgrounds nearby.
Seasons: June through October, or until the first snow falls!

WARD CREEK

The rides in this section all begin at the William Kent USFS campground.
Topo Maps: Tahoe City and Homewood 7.5 min., or Tahoe, CA 15 min. Ride starts from T15N, R16E, Section 24.
Water: Treated water is available at the campground. There are streams along several of the rides, but you'll need to filter or treat the water.

Ride #1 - The 21-Mile Spin!
Level of Difficulty: This is a fun ride for riders of all levels! Beginners will find the distance a challenge, while more advanced riders will enjoy going for a mountain bike ride in Tahoe where you can actually spin your pedals the entire ride! A lot of fun, pure and simple – a nice break from all the hard core climbing that many of the rides in the Tahoe area require.
Mileage: If you do both loops together this will be a 21-mile ride. Without the Paige Meadows Loop it is 16 miles.
Elevation: 6,250 ft. to 7,200 ft.

The Ride: 0.0 mile – From William Kent Campground, ride south on the bike path that follows Highway 89. 0.3 mile – Turn right on Pineland Drive. The road is marked by two poles with "Pineland" carved into them. 0.7 mile – Turn left on Twin Peaks Road following the sign to Ward Valley. Stay on the main road, which turns right and becomes Ward Creek Road. Three miles out, the name of the road changes to Courchevel Drive. Continue on into the beginning of a subdivision on the backside of Alpine Meadows Ski Area.

3.3 miles – Turn right on Chamonix Street. At the end of the street, your dirt riding begins. Climb up a short hill, and then go right on the main road marked 16N48. 4.7 miles – After you cross a creek – which may be dry by the end of the summer – stay on the main road that goes left. (Another trail takes off to the right and ties into the road and trail system near Paige Meadows, where you will end up towards the end of this ride.) 6.2 miles – A gradual climb is now over, and you ride along and above the Truckee River Canyon. Be sure to look over your right shoulder to get a glimpse of Lake Tahoe. The road will turn west, taking you through an old ski area. The next section of old road is almost level, giving you a chance to relax and enjoy the view down into Alpine Meadows, with the peaks of Squaw Valley and the Granite Chief Wilderness in the distance. Soon the road drops steeply into the canyon.

7.8 miles – As you are rapidly descending the road makes a sharp right turn. Continue downhill. 8.2 miles – The dirt road ends at a USFS green gate. Go around the gate and continue down Snow Crest, a paved road. 8.6 miles – Turn right on Alpine Meadows Road. 9.5 miles – Turn right on Highway 89, and look off to the right side of the road for the start of the bike trail. The bike trail takes you along a beautiful section of the Truckee River, quiet and peaceful in the early spring or fall. If you do this ride in mid-summer, however, the river may be bumper to bumper with rafts.

13.3 miles – In Tahoe city, turn right staying on Highway 89, and go across the bridge, staying on the bike path. There are plenty of places to stop for snacks along here. If you've had enough just stay on the bike path 2.5 miles back to the campground for a 16-mile loop. To ride the longer loop, turn right at the sign to Granlibakken Ski Resort (14.0 miles). 14.3 miles – Turn left on Rawhide Road, just before the entrance to Granlibakken. Ride 0.2 mile to the end of Rawhide, where the road turns to dirt. 15.4 miles – Stay right on the main road that makes a sharp right turn and continues to climb gradually. There will be several junctions along the next part of the ride, but just stay on the main road that climbs gradually, then turns west and continues straight ahead.

17.0 miles – You arrive at one of the Paige Meadows. At the beginning of the meadow, the road is blocked off by a large log and the area is posted *No Motor Vehicles*. Go around the log and ride out to Paige Meadows. There are several trails through and around the meadows. Continue heading west on the trail that take you from one meadow to the next, then turns into a road. 17.9 miles – Go straight and stay on the main road passing two roads on the right. Then get ready for a rocky downhill. 18.6 miles – Turn left on Ward Creek, the paved road. Follow it back to Pineland and down to Highway 89. Turn left to get back to the campground.

Ride #2 - Paige Meadows Loop
Level of Difficulty: This short ride is suitable for beginners and makes a perfect after-dinner ride for more advanced riders. (For a longer alternative, see Ride #1.)
Mileage: 10 miles.

Elevation: 6,250 ft. to 6,900 ft.

The Ride: 0.0 mile – From William Kent Campground, ride north on the bike trail along Highway 89. 2.0 miles – Turn left and follow the signs to Granlibakken Ski Resort. Just before you reach the resort turn left on Rawhide. Continue out until the road turns to dirt. 2.3 miles. – Turn left on Rawhide Road just before the entrance to Granlibakken. Ride 0.2 mile to the end of Rawhide where the road turns to dirt. You will be riding next to private land, so be sure to stay on the main road. 4.4 miles – Stay right as the road makes a sharp turn and continues to climb gradually. There will be several roads taking off through the next part of the ride. Stay on the main road that climbs gradually and then turns west.

6.0 miles – You arrive at Paige Meadows. At the beginning of the first meadow, the road is blocked by a large log and the area is posted *No Motor Vehicles.* Go around the log and ride out to Paige Meadows. Paige Meadows is actually several large meadows clustered together. In early summer they will be bright green, and if you visit them in fall the meadows will be a golden brown (Ward Peak is in the background). Be sure to stay on the main trails when riding in this area. The meadows are starting to recover after what looks like years of jeep traffic driving wildly across them. There are several trails through and around the meadows. Continue following the main trail that goes west through the meadows, then turns into a road.

6.9 miles – After exploring the meadow trails, make your way over to the road. Go straight on the main road past two roads leaving to your right. After the rocky downhill, turn left on paved Ward Creek. 7.6 miles – Follow this road back to Pineland and down to Highway 89. Turn left and ride the bike trail back to the campground.

Ride # 3 - Ward Creek
Level of Difficulty: Easy beginner ride. This is a good ride for a picnic along the creek. Beginners can rest at the creek while more adventurous riders can continue out the trail.
Mileage: 10.4 miles out and back.
Elevation: 6,250 ft. to 6,650 ft.

The Ride: 0.0 mile – William Kent Campground. Ride south 0.3 mile and turn right on Pineland Drive. 0.7 mile – Turn left on Twin Peaks Road and follow the sign to Ward Valley. Stay on the main road, which turns right and becomes Ward Creek Road. 2.2 miles – Turn left onto Upper Ward Creek (dirt road). After a short downhill it rolls along almost level to Upper Ward Creek. Several roads take off from the main road. Those to the right usually go back to the paved road, and the ones to the left go over towards Ward Creek and out into the meadow. 5.2 miles – The road ends at a *Road Closed* sign where the bridge across Ward Creek is gone. A trail continues on to the top of Twin Peaks from the other side of Ward Creek (see Ride #4). This ride ends here, so enjoy the creek and then follow your tracks back to the campground.

Ride #4 - Twin Peaks Bike and Hike

Level of Difficulty: Advanced level ride suitable only for those looking for an adventure. Everyone will push or hike parts of this route, but at any point you can turn around and ride back down to Ward Creek.
Mileage: 16 miles out and back.
Elevation: 6,250 ft. to 8,878 ft.

The Ride: 0.0 mile – From William Kent Campground, follow the directions in Ride #3 the first 5.2 miles to Upper Ward Creek. 5.2 miles – Go around the *Road Closed* sign and cross the creek to continue by mountain bike up the trail to Twin Peaks. The route starts off as an old jeep road, then turns into a single-track trail as it begins to climb up out of the valley. The trail is rough and suitable only for adventurous types, since it climbs about 1,900 feet in 2.6 miles. This may also be a ride where you choose to go as far as possible and then hide your bike for the final hike to the top of Twin Peaks. 7.8 miles – Once on top enjoy the view of Lake Tahoe to the east and Granite Chief Wilderness Area to the west. Hike back to where you left your bike and have fun on the downhill back to Ward Creek. On your way you may see another trail taking off toward the ridge to the east. This is an alternate way down that will take you to Stafford Rock and a jeep road that returns to Ward Creek. (We never tried it, but we heard it was rideable.) Both downhill routes take you back to Ward Creek Road. Turn right and continue out to Highway 89. Turn left onto the bike trail to get back to the campground.

BLACKWOOD CANYON

The Blackwood Canyon OHV Area is the site of a large meadow restoration project. A gravel quarry in the past, it is now being returned to its natural state and is impressive – already wildflowers are returning!

To get to this area, ride or drive on Highway 89 to Kaspian Picnic and Bicycle Campground, just north of Tahoe Pines. Turn west on Blackwood Canyon Road which is marked with large SNO-PARK signs. Follow the signs to the OHV Area two miles out. Turn right on the gravel road into the OHV Staging Area, where you will find parking, restrooms and a picnic area. This is a good spot to start riding if you have a large group with many cars.

Topo Maps: Homewood and Wentworth Springs 7.5 min., or Tahoe and Granite Chief 15 min. All rides start from T14N, R16E, Section 34.
Water: Bring water with you; there is no treated water available in the Blackwood Canyon OHV Area. Stream water is available at Blackwood Canyon and Barker Creek out on the rides. Be sure to filter or treat all water from mountain streams.

From Blackwood Canyon OHV Area, everything is up. If you enjoy hill climbing, this is a good place for you to begin your rides which all start by climbing to the top of Barker Pass (7,700 ft.). Fortunately there are three options for getting there!

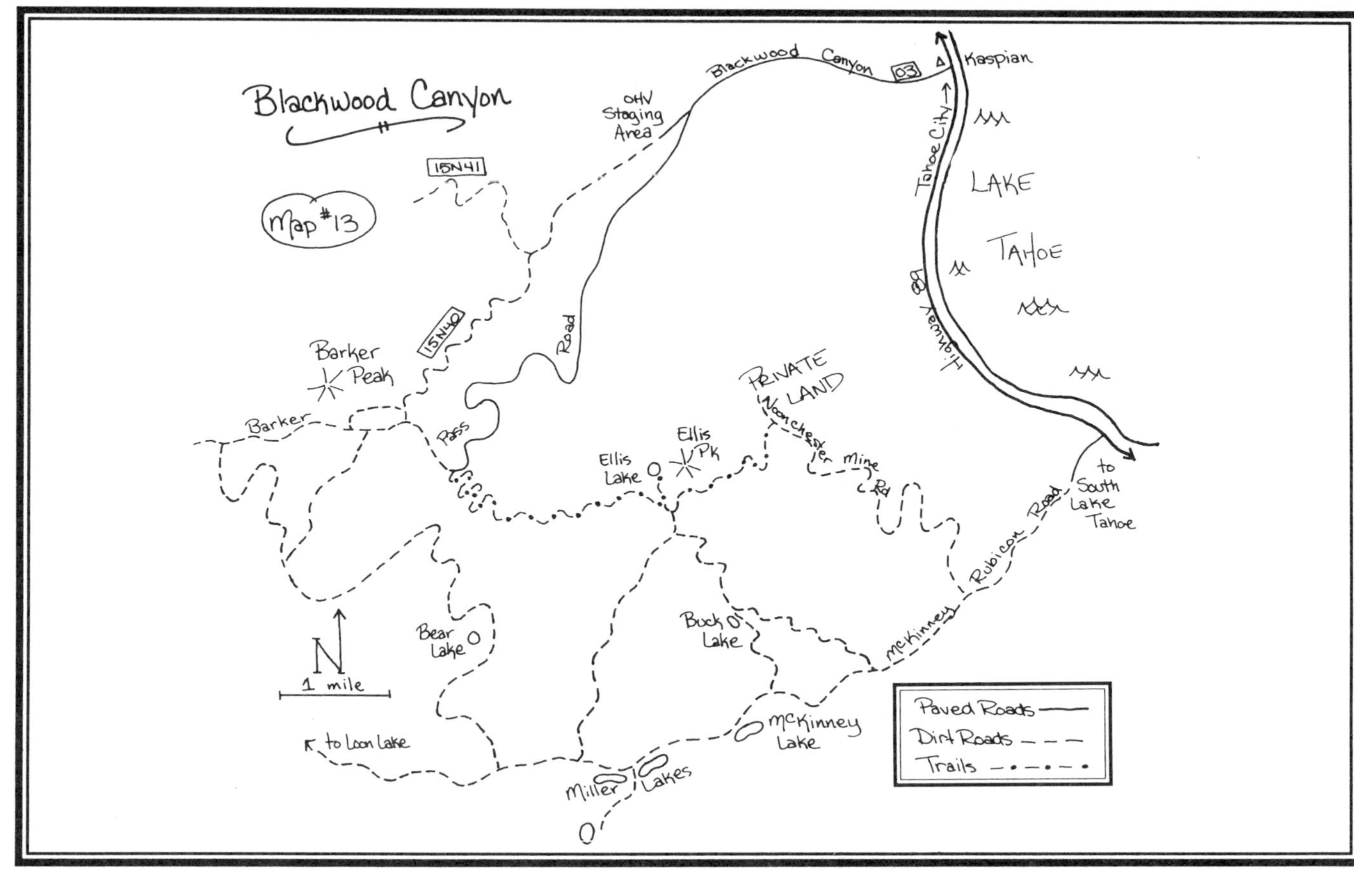

Blackwood Canyon
Map #13
15N41
15N40
OHV Staging Area
Blackwood Canyon
03
Kaspian
Tahoe City
Highway 89
LAKE
TAHOE
Road
Barker Peak
Barker
Pass
Ellis Lake
Ellis Pk
PRIVATE LAND
Wonchester Mine Rd
to South Lake Tahoe
Rubicon Road
McKinney
Buck O Lake
Bear Lake
N
1 mile
to Loon Lake
McKinney Lake
Miller Lakes
Paved Roads
Dirt Roads
Trails

Option A: From the OHV Area, continue west on the 4-wheel drive road, 15N40. At 0.8 mile out the road splits. Continue riding straight ahead on 15N40. (The road to the right – 15N41 – climbs out of the canyon and ends 3 miles out.) As your road leaves Blackwood Canyon it gets rougher and steeper, with sections that many will have to push. This is a tough climb, but it is only 3 miles to the top. Once on top, the peak to the right (west) is Barker Peak, behind it is Granite Chief Wilderness Area, and to the left is Ellis Peak. From Barker Pass, turn left on Barker Pass Road for Rides #5 or #6, or turn right for Ride #7.

Option B: From the OHV Area, ride back out to the paved road, turn right, and ride up to the top of Barker Pass. With this option, it is 5 miles to the top, paved all the way and with a much more gradual climb. When the pavement ends, Ride #5 and #6 continue out on the trail to your left. To get to Ride #7 continue straight ahead 0.5 mile.

Option C: If you have more than one vehicle in your group, you can do a shuttle, leaving one car at Blackwood Canyon OHV and driving to the top of Barker Pass in the other.

Ride # 5 - Ellis Peak Loop
Level of Difficulty: Intermediate or better riders. Most of this long all-day outing follows the route of the Tahoe Roubaix Race, known as one of the most challenging rides held in the Sierra. The elevation profile shows an overall gain of 2,000 feet, but because of terrain fluctuations you climb over 3,000 feet. The ride can be shortened and made easier by driving to the top of Barker Pass to start.
Mileage: 25 miles from the top of Barker Pass, or 29 miles if you start from Blackwood Canyon OHV Area.
Elevation: 6,400 ft. to 6,500 ft.

The Ride: 0.0 mile – From the Blackwood Canyon OHV Area, ride up road 15N40 to the top of Barker Pass. The mileage below assumes you chose to ride up 15N40 – Option A. If you use Options B or C, adjust your mileage accordingly. Add two miles if you ride the pavement, or subtract three miles if you drive to the top.

3.5 miles – Turn right on the motorcycle/hiking trail, which begins to climb immediately. If it hasn't rained in a while, the soil will be loose and most people will have to push through a series of switchbacks. Once on the ridge top, the trail becomes rideable again and you are treated to a magnificent view in all directions! The large lake to the southwest is Loon Lake, and if you look closely you will see Spider Lake and Buck Island Lake with Desolation Valley Wilderness Area in the distance. To the north is Blackwood Canyon, where you started your ride, and Lake Tahoe in the background.

5.5 miles – The trail ends at a road. To complete the loop turn right. (If you take a left, you can ride out to Ellis Lake 0.5 mile for a swim.) 5.7 miles – Turn left. The road begins the final ascent to Ellis Peak. (Ride #6 goes straight ahead here.) 6.0 miles – Turn left. Ride as far as you can, then walk the final 0.1 miles to the top of

Ellis Peak. Enjoy the view, then ride back down to the main road. 6.2 miles – Turn left. The road quickly becomes a trail and can be hard to follow. The trail you should be on stays on the north side of the ridge in front of you.

7.5 miles – When the trail ends at a dirt road, turn right on Noonchester Mine Road. This next section travels through private land, so be sure to stay on the road. Just after you cross Homewood Creek it's "Heads-Up" time: *Be on the look out for a cable across the road!* Negotiate the cable, then continue on. The road contours around the ridge, offering another great view of Lake Tahoe. Quail Lake is right below you. After you've enjoyed the view, prepare for the last three miles of wild downhill. *Warning! This next section of road is listed on the Tahoe Basin OHV handout, so be prepared for uphill traffic around every turn!*

10.5 miles – When you cross McKinney Creek, the downhill is over for a while. Turn right on McKinney-Rubicon Road. 11.8 miles – Continue straight ahead. (The steep road to the left goes to Buck Lake and then back up the hill to Ellis Peak). 13.0 miles – Off to your left is McKinney Lake. Continue on and pass by Lily Lake. Then the road begins to level out and you arrive at the first Miller Lake. 15.0 miles – Go straight past the second Miller Lake, where a road takes off to the left. This road goes to Richardson Lake and then down to Sugar Pine Point State Park. (For more information on rides to the south see *Mountain Biking the High Sierra, Guide 3A.)*

15.6 miles – Continue straight when a road enters from the right. (It is the road you come down in Ride #6.) 16.1 miles – Turn right when the road forks. (Left takes you out the Rubicon Jeep Trail that goes all the way to Loon Lake, an area described in *Guide 3A.)* Climb to the top of the ridge and get ready for a fast downhill as the road circles around Bear Lake before climbing again.

20.5 miles – The road crosses Barker Creek. If you are out of water fill up here; there's one more climb to go. (Be sure to filter or treat the water). Ride across the creek, then take the road to the immediate right. It follows along Barker Meadows, through private land, and then to the final climb of the trip. 22.5 miles – You arrive back on top of Barker Pass. If you are tired, take the paved road back down to the OHV Area. If you want to ride more rough stuff, go across Barker Pass Road and take 15N40 instead.

Ride #6 - Miller Lake Loop

Level of Difficulty: Advanced level ride that climbs 1,800 feet and then descends on a fast, rough road. The views are spectacular!
Mileage: 20 miles (24 if you ride the paved road up to Barker Pass in both directions).
Elevation: 6,400 ft. to 8,200 ft.

The Ride: 0.0 mile – From the Blackwood Canyon OHV Area follow Ride #5 for the first 5.7 miles. 5.7 miles – Continue past the turn-off to Ellis Peak. Stay on the main road that starts downhill quickly, then levels off as you ride through a large meadow near North Miller Creek. If your hands are sore from squeezing the brakes, rest here; once you leave the meadow the road gets rough and drops steeply down to Miller Lake.

8.7 miles – The road ends at McKinney-Rubicon Road. Turn right.(Miller Lake is a short distance to the left.) 9.7 miles – The road forks. Turn right and begin climbing to the top of the ridge. Then it is time for a fast downhill as the road circles around Bear Lake before climbing again. 14.1 miles – You cross Barker Creek, then take the immediate road to the right. This follows along Barker Meadows (through private land) before you begin the final climb. 16.6 miles – You arrive back on top of Barker Pass. If you are tired, take the paved road down to the OHV Area, but if you want to ride more dirt, go across Barker Pass Road and take 15N40 instead.

Ride #7 - Barker Pass Loop

Level of Difficulty: Intermediate level ride. This is the easiest ride from Blackwood Canyon OHV Area, staying entirely on wide dirt roads, but there is still 1,300 feet of climbing.
Mileage: 12 miles (16 miles if you ride the pavement to and from Barker Pass).
Elevation: 6,400 ft. to 7,700 ft.

The Ride: 0.0 mile – From the Blackwood Canyon OHV Area, ride to the top of Barker Pass using any of the three options described in Ride #5. The mileage below assumes you chose to ride up 15N40, the dirt road. Be sure to adjust your mileage if you go up another way.

3.0 miles – From Barker Pass, ride across the main road and look for a road going down the other side. The Pacific Crest Trail also crosses here, but it is closed to bicycle use. Stay on the main road as it goes quickly downhill and levels out close to a meadow. Then follow along Barker Creek until the road ends at 5.0 miles. Turn right. The road begins to climb gradually at first, but it gets steeper as you work your way up into logging country. Logging roads take off at several places; stay on the main road with two wide switchbacks that take you back up to Barker Pass Road.

7.3 miles – Turn right on Barker Pass Road and ride back to Barker Pass. The rocky peaks to the southwest are in Desolation Wilderness Area, and Barker Peak is straight ahead. 8.6 miles – The shortest way down from Barker Pass is to take 15N40, the dirt road heading to the left. For a gentler descent stay on the main road which turns to pavement. Both take you back down to the OHV area.

CHAPTER 9   NORTH SHORE LAKE TAHOE
Tahoe City to Truckee; Antone Meadows Loop; Watson Lake Loop; Watson Lake Loop from Dollar Point; Martis Peak Lookout; Mt. Baldy Loop; Watson Lake from Brockway Summit; Northstar Ski Area

This chapter has something for riders of all abilities: included are a ride to a secluded mountain lake, a lookout ride, a special section on riding the cross-country ski trails at Northstar Ski Area, and the Tahoe to Truckee Ride – one of the oldest mountain bike races held in the Sierra.

This is also timber country with endless miles of logging roads to explore. You will be riding through sections of private timber company lands, so always stay on the main roads and obey *No Trespassing* signs. Watch out for logging trucks.

Nearest Services: Tahoe City, Truckee and Kings Beach.
Campgrounds: Several campgrounds are located nearby, and you can do the rides right from your campsite. The Tahoe State Recreation Area and Lake Forest are near Tahoe City. Along Highway 89 there are three US Forest Service camp-grounds: Granite Flat, Goose Meadow and Silver Creek.
Seasons: Mid-June through October.

TAHOE TO TRUCKEE

Ride #1 - Tahoe City to Truckee
This ride follows the route of The Tahoe City to Truckee Race. For those who have never tried a mountain bike race and would like to, this is a good one to begin your career. Most of the route is on good surface dirt and gravel roads, with one small section of wide single-track. It is also used in winter for a cross-country ski race.

Riders usually begin at North Lake Tahoe High School, but it is also convenient to start from the campgrounds and ride your bike to the school.

Topo Maps: Tahoe City and Truckee 7.5 min., or Truckee and Tahoe 15 min. Rides start at T16N, R17E, Section 3.
Level of Difficulty: Intermediate, but if you choose to do the entire 40 miles, you should be in good shape physically and accustomed to riding all day. Most of the climbing is on good surface dirt roads; nothing too technical, but a very long ride.
Elevation: 6,250 ft. to 7,800 ft.
Mileage: One way from Tahoe City to Truckee is 19 miles; loop ride 40 miles.
Water: Carry all that you will need. Water is not available on the trail.

Comments: If you ride the entire 40-mile loop, you will ride 19 miles of dirt and 21 miles of pavement. Most people enjoy it more as a one-way ride with a car shuttle. A good place to leave your vehicle is where Forest Road 06 starts at Thelin Drive, or somewhere within the town of Truckee. (Truckee is usually full of tourists every day of the week during summer, and parking is at a premium in Old Town Truckee.) To get to Forest Road 06 from Truckee, drive southeast on Highway 267 and turn right on Palisades Road. Continue on until the road becomes Ponderosa Drive. Turn right on Silver Fir Drive and left onto Thelin Drive. Look off to your left for a green gate at the beginning of Forest Road 06. Park here without blocking the road.

In Tahoe City, start from the intersection of Highway 89 and Highway 28. Ride or drive northeast on Highway 28 through the main part of town. Turn left (northwest) on Old Mill Road, and after about a half mile, turn left again on Polaris at the top of the hill. Continue 0.4 mile farther to the end of the pavement just past North Lake Tahoe High School. If you drove to this point, park here out of the way of the school traffic.

The Ride: 0.0 mile – Ride out the dirt road that begins where the pavement ends and you enter Burton Creek State Park. Stay on the main road that leads through the forest and heads over towards Antone Meadows and Burton Creek. 0.3 mile – Stay left, then take an immediate right on the main road. 1.1 miles – Go straight, staying on the main road. 1.9 miles – When you arrive at a fork in the road, go right. You will be riding along the far edge of Antone Meadows. (The road to the left leads over to Antone Meadows and a small dam before it loops around and rejoins the road you are on.)

2.6 miles – At the upper end of the meadow, you ride through a big curve. Take the next right on a road that goes uphill, out of Burton Creek State Park. As you leave the Park, the road turns into a wide single-track trail and begins to climb. The single-track climbs quickly and can sometimes be loose and difficult to ride. But if you hit it just after a thunder shower, the traction is great and the entire mile of single-track is rideable. Be aware that this is a two-way road and you may encounter downhill traffic. Stay alert at all times! 3.6 miles – The single-track ends in a switchback turn on Forest Road 16N73. Go right and continue climbing towards the top of Mt. Watson. 4.5 miles – The Tahoe Rim Trail crosses the road. 4.7 miles – Stay on the main road where another road takes off to the left. You pass a sign facing in the downhill direction: *Tahoe City 3 Miles.* 5.8 miles – As the road contours around the north side of the ridge, another road enters from the right. Go straight.

6.7 miles – You reach a junction, and are done with the majority of the climbing! Take a left here on Forest Road 06 and prepare for the downhill section of the ride. (Straight ahead 6 miles is Brockway Summit on State Highway 267.) As you descend Forest Road 06, it stays wide and is not very technical. Just watch for gravel and sharp turns. Continue on this main road. This is logging country, so there are roads taking off all over the place. The main route is also a snowmobile and cross-country ski route, so you'll see orange diamonds and snowmobile signs marked *Forest Road 06.* You ride along the boundary of Northstar Ski Area, then through a large plantation of trees. After 10+ miles of mostly downhill, the dirt road ends at a large gate.

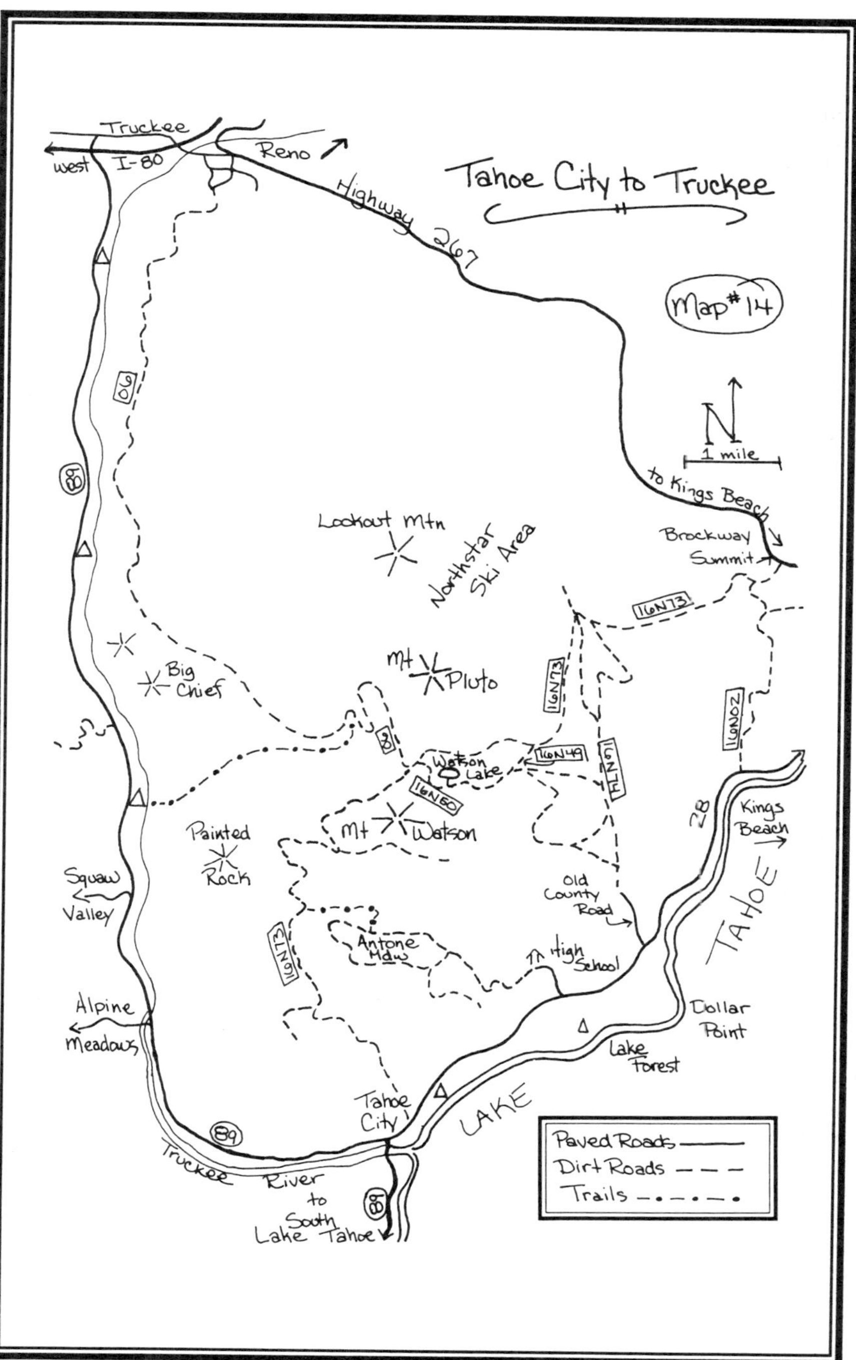

Tahoe City to Truckee
Map #14
Truckee
west   I-80
Reno
Highway 267
N
1 mile
to Kings Beach
Brockway Summit
06
89
Lookout Mtn
Northstar Ski Area
16N73
16N73
16N02
Mt Pluto
89
16N49
16N74
Watson Lake
Big Chief
16N50
28
Kings Beach
Painted Rock
Mt Watson
TAHOE
Squaw Valley
Old County Road
16N73
Antone Mdw
High School
Alpine Meadows
Dollar Point
Lake Forest
Tahoe City
LAKE
89
Truckee River
to South Lake Tahoe
89
Paved Roads
Dirt Roads
Trails

17.5 miles – Turn left on the paved road (Thelin Drive). You are now in a subdivision of Truckee. At the next intersection turn right on Silver Fir Drive. From here you can ride straight ahead on the pavement to get to downtown Truckee, or you can take a left on Aspenwood for a short single-track down to town. If you choose Aspenwood, ride to the end of the pavement and continue out the rocky road. Just before the road reaches the power line, turn left down a trail. Go right at the next intersection and continue down the rocky trail. When you reach the edge of town, you can go left to Hill Top Restaurant, or go right to Pine Cone Drive. Either way, you need to continue downhill to the old part of Truckee and State Route 267.

To do this ride as a loop, continue into town, cross the railroad tracks, and turn left. *(Watch out for tourists backing up their cars without looking!)* You might want to get off your bike and walk along the sidewalk for a bit of window shopping. If you are hungry or thirsty, you should have no problem satisfying those needs. Old Town Truckee is a fun place to explore if you have the time.

When you are ready to continue, you have two choices:
A: Stay on the main road that crosses under Interstate 80 and goes through a newer section of Truckee. When you reach Highway 89, turn left and follow the signs to Tahoe City. The bike lane starts here.

B: (The dirt route.) Ride the gravel road along the railroad tracks. When you reach the sign that reads *No Trespassing Beyond This Point,* turn right on the dirt road that goes up and over the hill. There are actually several roads that will work. Just remember to keep climbing. Then continue down the other side to where the dirt road ends at the intersection of Highway 89 and Interstate 80. Carefully cross the highway and turn left. You have now travelled 22 miles. If you are thirsty stop here, since the next store is 9 miles farther. For the next section of the ride, you travel on a bike lane along Highway 89, with a lot of traffic all the way to the Alpine Meadows turnoff. This can be incredibly noisy!

31 miles – You reach the turnoff to Squaw Valley, with a handy 7-11 store if you need a break from riding the pavement. 33 miles – From the turnoff to Alpine Meadows, the bike trail leaves the highway, and it is quite enjoyable to ride along the Truckee River. This is also a great route for people watching, with many people riding along the bike path or floating down the Truckee River. 37 miles – The good bike trail ends at the intersection of Highway 89 and Highway 28. Turn left on Highway 28 and ride through Tahoe City. 39 miles – Turn left on Old Mill Road and ride the last uphill back to your car at 40.0 miles.

Ride #2 - Antone Meadows Loop
Level of Difficulty: Easy beginner ride; also a perfect short ride for after dinner. Suitable for small children and others who are just learning how to use their bikes.
Mileage: 6.4 miles.
Elevation: 6,250 ft. to 6,840 ft.

The Ride: 0.0 mile – From North Lake Tahoe High School (see Ride #1 for directions), ride out the dirt road that begins where the pavement ends. You will be entering Burton Creek State Park. Stay on the main road that leads through the forest and heads over towards Antone Meadows and Burton Creek. 0.3 miles – Stay left, then take an immediate right on the main road. 1.1 miles – Go straight, staying on the main road. 1.9 miles – When you arrive at a fork in the road (the road on which you 'll return), go right and ride along the far edge of Antone Meadows.

2.6 miles – You ride through a big curve at the upper end of the meadow. Stay on the main road that loops around the meadow. (Ride #1 takes off to the right from this point.) 4.3 miles – Turn left and continue to the dam on Burton Creek. If you do this ride in June or July, the wildflowers can be incredible! After exploring, continue on. 4.5 miles – You have completed the loop. Turn right and follow your tracks back to your car.

Ride #3 - Watson Lake Loop
Level of Difficulty: Strong beginner to easy intermediate.
Mileage: 17.5 miles.
Elevation: 6,250 ft. to 7,800 ft.
Comments: Watson Lake is a quiet spot most of the time, although the campsites look well used. We camped here one night and were amazed at how peaceful it was with the Tahoe summer traffic only 7 miles away! This is a great spot to camp and do some exploring. There are roads everywhere. If you decide to camp here, you need a campfire permit. For exploring, come equipped with a compass, topo maps, an OHV map and a Forest Service map. A helpful hint to remember is that, as a rule, most road numbers ending with 00 go somewhere, and the ones ending with a number like 05 and 13 are usually dead-end roads.

The Ride: 0.0 mile – Start from North Lake Tahoe High School and follow the directions given in Ride #1 to the intersection with Forest Road 06 and the main road to Truckee. 6.7 miles – Continue straight ahead on Road 16N73, Mt. Watson Road (6 miles to State Highway 267 at Brockway Summit). 7.0 miles – Turn right at a road marked by a stake with *6/30* on it. (This road is designated on OHV maps as Road 16N50). 7.6 miles – Watson Lake. Enjoy the solitude of the lake, take a swim and relax before continuing on. When you are ready to leave, follow the road that heads east away from the lake. After riding over a small hill, the road begins to descend rapidly. This is a rough and rocky downhill section. You pass a couple of roads that take off to the right, but stay on the main road.

8.4 miles – Turn left on road 16N49. It heads through Watson Creek Meadow and then gradually climbs back to Mt. Watson Road (also know as 16N73 or Road 100). 8.8 miles – Turn left onto Mt. Watson Road. As it climbs back onto the ridge, be sure to look behind and to your left for a great view of Lake Tahoe. 10.8 miles – The Watson Lake Loop is complete and you are back at the intersection of Road 06. Continue straight ahead and follow your tracks back down to your car. *Caution: While you ride down the single-track trail, watch out for uphill traffic!* (If you miss the turn onto the single-track, 16N73 continues on and ends up in Tahoe City in a subdivision behind the golf course.)

Ride #4 - Watson Lake Loop from Dollar Point

Topo Maps: Tahoe City and Kings Beach 7.5 min., or Tahoe 15 min. Ride starts at T16N, R17E, Section 33.
Level of Difficulty: Intermediate level ride with a good climb in the beginning.
Mileage: 13 miles, or 15 miles if you start in Tahoe City.
Elevation: 6,250 ft. to 7,800 ft.

Ride or drive northeast on Highway 28, going 2.6 miles past Tahoe City. Turn left on Old County Road at Dollar Point. Stay on Old County Road until the pavement ends at Beverly Road, 0.8 mile farther. If you drove, park your car here.

The Ride: 0.0 mile – Ride out dirt road 16N74, located at the end of the pavement to the right of a house. As you climb away from the lake, you pass several roads entering from the left. Most of them are alternate routes down from the top of the ridge. Just continue on the main road 16N74 to the top of the ridge. 3.2 miles –The road ends at Sawmill Flat. Turn left on Mt. Watson Road 16N73, and continue to climb up the ridge to Mt. Watson. In places it is steep and washboarded from logging trucks, but it is still rideable.

4.7 miles – Forest Road 16N49 takes off to the left. This is the road you will return on, but it is better to continue straight ahead and get all of the climbing over first. 6.4 miles – Turn left at a road marked *6/30* – 16N50 on the OHV maps. (If you arrive at a major intersection with Road 06, you went 0.3 miles too far.) 7.0 miles – Watson Lake. When you are ready to continue, head east on the road that leaves the lake. 7.8 miles – Turn left on road 16N49. This road goes through Watson Creek Meadows and gradually climbs back to road 16N73. 8.2 miles – Turn right on 16N73 and follow the tracks back to your car.

BROCKWAY SUMMIT

Riding in the Brockway Summit area is similar to the other spots around Lake Tahoe in that all of the routes involve a fair amount of climbing. But once on top, the rewards of spectacular views and exciting downhills make for wonderful riding terrain.

All of the rides described in this section start from Brockway Summit on Highway 267 between Kings Beach and Truckee. From Kings Beach – on the north shore of Lake Tahoe – drive north on Highway 267 to the top of Brockway Summit. As you start down the east side, look off to your right (north) for a dirt road marked *18N02*. Park here or drive in a bit if you want to shorten the rides and cut down on the amount of climbing you will do.

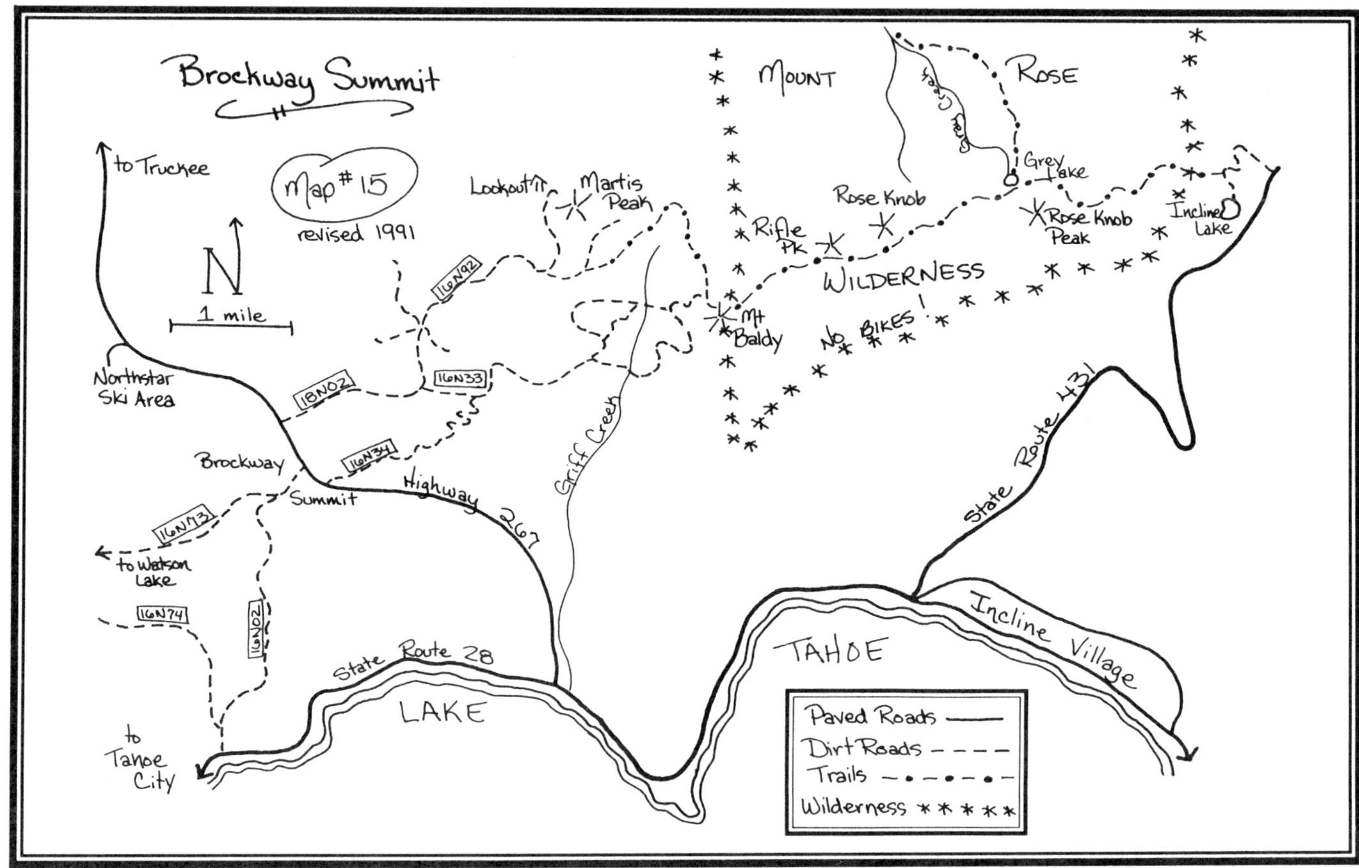

Brockway Summit
Map #15
revised 1991
N
1 mile
to Truckee
to Watson Lake
to Tahoe City
Northstar Ski Area
Brockway Summit
16N13
16N74
16N02
16N02
16N31
16N33
16N92
Highway 267
State Route 28
LAKE
TAHOE
Griff Creek
Lookout Martis Peak
Mt Baldy
Rifle Pk
Rose Knob
WILDERNESS
No BIKES!
Mount
ROSE
Gray Creek
Grey Lake
Rose Knob Peak
Incline Lake
Incline Village
State Route 431
Paved Roads
Dirt Roads
Trails
Wilderness

Topo Maps: Martis Peak and Mt. Rose 7.5 min., or Truckee and Mt. Rose 15 min. Rides start from T16N, R17E, Section 3.
Seasons: June through October.
Nearest Services: Kings Beach.

Ride #5 – Martis Peak Lookout
Level of Difficulty: Suitable for intermediates and strong beginners who enjoy a good climb. This ride is like most lookout rides – up on the way in and down on the way back out.
Mileage: 6 miles out and back.
Elevation: 7,150 ft. to 8,656 ft.
Water: Bring all that you will need; many of the creeks will be dry by mid-summer.

The Ride: 0.0 mile – From Highway 267, ride out road 18N02. Stay on the main road that climbs steep at first and then becomes a more gradual climb. (The main roads in this area are marked with cross-country ski diamonds for winter use.) 1.3 miles – Go left on the main road. (The road straight ahead is 16N33.) 1.9 miles – At a five-way intersection, stay on the main road that continues to climb. 3.3 miles – The road reaches the ridge top. Take a left here to finish the final climb to the lookout tower.

3.9 miles – Martis Peak Lookout (elev. 8,656 ft.) To the north are Donner Lake, Prosser Lake, Boca Reservoirs and Dry Lake. To the south you can see all of Lake Tahoe! To the west is Mt. Watson, Mt. Pluto and Northstar Ski Area. For a better view to the east, ride or walk the final 100 feet to the top of Martis Peak. When you are done enjoying the view, prepare for the wild descent and follow your tracks back to your car. (For a longer ride, turn left, instead of right, at the first intersection and follow the directions for Ride #6 below.)

Ride #6 - Mt. Baldy Loop
Level of Difficulty: Strong intermediate or better, due to the amount of climbing and the single-track. This ride can be done in both directions, and it is hard to say which way the climb is easiest or the downhill more fun.
Mileage: 12.6 miles.
Elevation: 7,150 ft. to 9,100 ft.
Water: Bring all that you will need, since many of the creeks will be dry by mid-summer.

The Ride: 0.0 mile – Start at road 18N02 on Highway 267. Follow Ride #5, Martis Peak Lookout, for the first 3.3 miles. Continue straight ahead instead of turning left to go to the lookout. 3.9 miles (0.6 mile from the lookout intersection) – Take an old jeep road off to the right (more like a trail than a road). There is a rock painted lavender in the middle of the trail, and orange flagging hanging in a tree at the start. Follow this old road all the time. You may have to push in spots. 4.7 miles – At a fork, go right and continue climbing and pushing to the top of the first ridge.

5.2 miles – The trail becomes a jeep road and stays fairly level for a short while, then it begins to climb. 6.6 miles – Stay left, continuing the climb up the ridge.

6.8 miles – Turn left here to go to the top of Mt. Baldy for another great view of Lake Tahoe. (This is the intersection you will be returning to after climbing to the top.) 7.2 miles – Look off to the left for a yellow sign (a "K-tag") on a tree that marks the boundary between California and Nevada. Welcome to Nevada! 7.3 miles – Lay down your bike, and hike out to the edge to enjoy the 360° view! When you are ready to ride again, return to the last intersection 0.4 mile back. You are on the edge of the Wilderness Area at this point. If you want to continue to Gray Lake you must leave your bike and hike in.

7.7 miles. Turn left at the intersection this time and prepare for a long downhill stretch. Stay left on the main road past the first four junctions. At times you will feel like you are losing too much elevation and that you are going to end up in Lake Tahoe, but you can enjoy over 2 miles of downhill before you need to turn. From the map, it appears that other roads to the right will also take you back to the Martis Peak Lookout Road. Just be careful, because this is one of those places with roads going everywhere! 10.5 miles – Turn right. The road flattens out before climbing just a bit. 11.3 miles – Road 16N33 ends at the Martis Peak Road. Stay on the main road to return to your car.

Ride #7 - Watson Lake from Brockway Summit
Topo Maps: Tahoe City and Kings Beach 7.5 min., or Tahoe and Truckee 15 min.
Ride starts from T16N, R17E, Section 3.
Level of Difficulty: Beginner ride. All on wide dirt or gravel roads.
Mileage: 11.5 miles out and back.
Elevation: 7,200 ft. to 7,800 ft.
Water: None available; carry all that you will need.

This ride starts on the Mt. Watson Road (16N73), a dirt road that goes west from the top of Brockway Summit.

The Ride: 0.0 mile – Ride southwest on Mt. Watson Road. It is primarily gravel and climbs 600 feet right at the beginning, but it is not a difficult road to ride. 2.7 miles out you reach Sawmill Flats and Forest Road 16N74. Continue straight ahead and climb up the ridge towards Mt. Watson. It is steep in places and washboarded from logging truck traffic, but it is still rideable. 4.2 miles – Forest Road 16N49 takes off to the left. This is the road you will return on, but you may as well continue straight ahead and get all of the climbing over first.

5.9 miles. Turn left at the road marked *6/30* – 16N50 on the OHV maps. (If you arrive at a major intersection with Road 06, you went 0.3 miles too far.) 6.5 miles – Watson Lake. When you are ready to continue, head east on the road that leaves the lake. 7.3 miles – Turn left on road 16N49, which goes through Watson Creek Meadows and gradually climbs back to 16N73. 8.2 miles – Turn right on 16N73 and follow your tracks back to the car.

NORTHSTAR SKI AREA

When you are planning a trip to North Tahoe, another spot worth checking out is Northstar Ski Area, located just off Highway 267 between Kings Beach and Truckee. Northstar is a year-round recreation area with downhill and cross-country skiing in winter, and a wide variety of summer activities such as tennis, horseback riding, swimming, hiking and mountain biking. The cross-country ski trails are open to mountain bikes, and from these trails there is good access to the surrounding National Forest. Riding from Northstar, you can tie into the road system by Mt. Watson.

When you arrive at the main village center at Northstar, you should check at the Outpost Store for a trail map and current information on which trails are open and which are closed to riders. (Please check, since areas are occasionally closed due to chairlift construction or work on the ski slopes.) The Outpost Store rents a variety of mountain bikes, offers daily introductory mountain bike lessons, and has information about other events it sponsors (guided lunch tours, shuttles to the top of the mountain, and Mountain Bike Weekend packages). We found the person in the store quite friendly and knowledgeable about mountain biking — not just in Northstar, but in nearby areas also. For more information, call the Outpost Store at (916) 562-1010.

Maps: Use the maps provided by Northstar. If you are riding outside of the area or would like more detailed information, use these topo maps: Truckee, Tahoe City, Kings Beach and Martis Peak 7.5 min., or Tahoe 15 min. Northstar is located at T16N, R17E, Section 7.

Level of Difficulty: The cross-country ski trails are rated according to their length and level of difficulty. Riders of all skill levels will find suitable routes here.

Water: Water is available at Northstar.

Nearest Services: Small stores and deli restaurants are located in the main center at Northstar. The Outpost Store currently does not supply bicycle parts; the closest bike shops are in Kings Beach or Truckee.

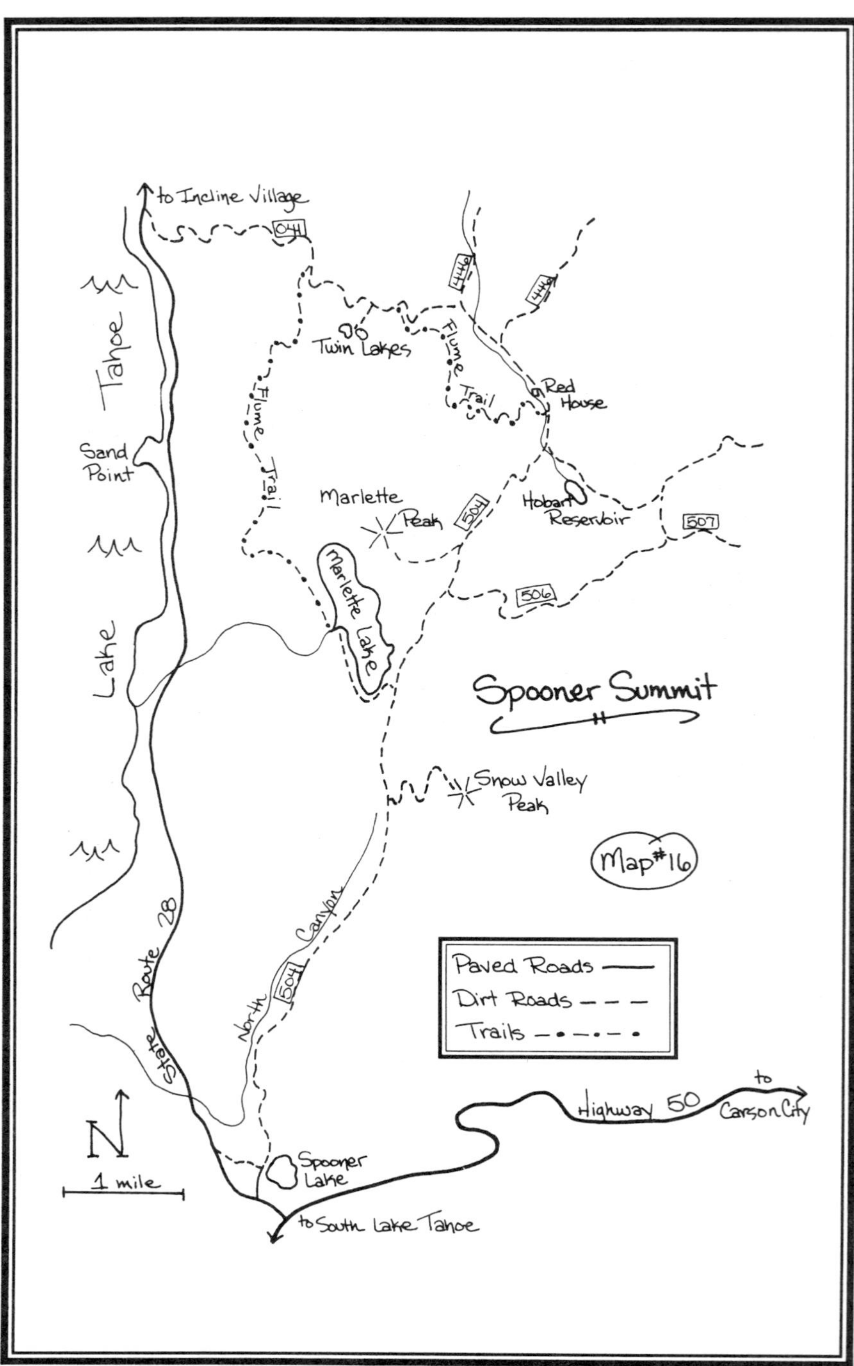

to Incline Village
041
447
444
Tahoe
Twin Lakes
Flume Trail
Red House
Sand Point
Flume Trail
Marlette
Peak
504
Hobart Reservoir
507
Lake
Marlette Lake
506
Spooner Summit
Snow Valley Peak
Map #16
North Canyon
504
State Route 28
Paved Roads
Dirt Roads
Trails
N
1 mile
Highway 50
to Carson City
Spooner Lake
to South Lake Tahoe

CHAPTER 10   NORTHEAST SHORE LAKE TAHOE
Marlette Lake; The Great Flume Ride; Hobart Reservoir Loop; Ophir Creek Trail; Mt. Rose Relay Station

The group of rides described in this chapter are located in the eastern portion of the Sierra Nevada in what is known as the Carson Range. On the eastern side of the Sierra the climate is much more arid, with fewer densely forested areas and more high alpine sage groundcover.

The main highways here are State Route 28 along the northeast shore of Lake Tahoe, Mt. Rose Highway (431) connecting Incline Village to Reno, and Highway 50, to the south. (For rides south of Highway 50, see *Guide 3A*.)

One section of this chapter is devoted to Lake Tahoe / Nevada State Park where you will find the route description for one of the most well known rides in the Tahoe area, The Great Flume Ride. This is a "must do" ride for those with intermediate or better riding skills. The single-track portion is a challenge, and the views are incredible!

Camping: The only campgrounds in this area are located on the Mt. Rose Highway. Bike-in and wilderness campsites are available in Lake Tahoe / Nevada State Park at Spooner Lake. Other than the wilderness campsites, the State Park is for day-use only.
Seasons: June through October. This is a spectacular place to ride in the fall! The east side of the Sierra has large aspen groves which turn bright yellow to orange around the first of October.
Nearest Services: Incline Village or South Lake Tahoe will probably have everything you need in the way of food, restaurants, lodging and bike shops.

SPOONER SUMMIT

To get to Spooner Summit from South Lake Tahoe, drive northeast on U.S. 50 about 12 miles past the casinos and turn left on Nevada State Highway 28. Continue north for about a half mile before turning right into Nevada State Park at Spooner Lake. (From the North Shore of Lake Tahoe, take Nevada State Highway 28 south from Incline Village. Just before the junction of Highway 28 and U.S. 50, turn left into Nevada State Park.

The State Park is a day-use facility, and it is certainly worth the $3.00 entry fee to park your car inside ($1.00 fee if you enter by bike). This area is currently closed to motor vehicles (except Park vehicles), including motorcycles, and there have been rumors of possibly closing it to mountain bikes. Injured people who can't ride out have to be evacuated by Park personnel, and unfortunately this happens several times each summer. Also, many riders park outside the gate and ride in without paying. Money is spent on the Park's trail system to maintain it for everyone, and mountain bikers need to start paying their fair share. If you choose to ride in this

This State Park is rich in history. The Spooner Lake area was used by the Washoe Indians as a camp, and during the 1870s it was a central point in the route for transporting wood from Glenbrook (on the shore of Lake Tahoe) to Virginia City. If you are interested in local history, pick up a brochure when you enter the Park.

Topo Maps: Marlette Lake and Glenbrook 7.5 min., or Carson City 15 min. All rides in this section start from within the picnic area at Spooner Lake at T14N, R18E, Section 12.

Ride #1 - Marlette Lake
Level of Difficulty: Strong beginner to intermediate. If you are unsure whether or not you can do the Flume Ride you should plan to do this one first as a trial.
Mileage: 12.5 miles out and back.
Elevation: 7,000 ft. to 8,157 ft.

The Ride: 0.0 mile – Go east out of the picnic area towards Spooner Lake. Turn left (north) on the dirt road that heads toward the big meadow. The road continues along North Canyon Creek and the edge of the meadow. It then begins climbing up towards Marlette Lake, passing an old cattle grazers cabin built in the 1920s. 2.8 miles – You reach the first of the backcountry campgrounds. Continue straight ahead. 3.9 miles – Continue straight ahead to go to Marlette Lake. To the right is road 15N04A, which takes you to the top of Snow Valley Peak (elev. 9,214 ft.) after 1.5 miles of climbing. It's a steep, steady climb with an incredible view from the top!)

4.2 miles – At elevation 8,157 feet, the climbing is over! Enjoy the 0.6 mile descent to Marlette Lake. When you arrive, turn left and follow the road that goes around the shore. Marlette Lake is used as a breeding area for cutthroat trout, and there is a small hatchery at the inlet on the south end of the lake. No fishing is allowed. 6.2 miles – You arrive at the dam. (A left turn would take you on the Flume Ride.) This ride ends here, so rest and enjoy the view before following your tracks back. *Caution: Be sure to ride carefully down the hill! Be on the lookout for hikers, horseback riders, and other cyclists making their way up. The turns can be loose and sandy, so control your speed at all times!*

Ride #2 - The Great Flume Ride
This is one of the true "classic" Tahoe rides, a technical ride with magnificent views the entire way! You ride single-track trail on the abandoned flume line that follows the east side of Lake Tahoe, a thousand vertical feet above the lake.
Level of Difficulty: Strong intermediate or better; a technical ride, this is only for those with prior trail riding experience. Done as a tour the ride takes most riders all day to complete.
Mileage: 23 miles.
Elevation: 7,000 ft. to 8,300 ft.

Water: Good water is available in the Picnic Area at Spooner Lake. There are several spots along the way to get water from creeks and lakes, but it must be filtered or treated.

The Ride: 0.0 mile – Starting from Spooner Lake Picnic Area go north on the dirt road following the directions for Ride #1 to Marlette Lake. Continue to the dam. 6.2 miles – Look off to the left end of the dam (southeast) for the sign: *Flume Trail.* Carefully ride down a short, steep, sandy stretch with a sharp right turn at the bottom. Continue across Marlette Creek and you are on the Flume Trail. It is a narrow trail contouring along the ridge at 7,700 feet, 1,500 vertical feet above Lake Tahoe! ***Caution:*** *Do not attempt this trail if you are afraid of heights or have not done much trail riding with your bike!* The trail is not that difficult, but it is not a beginner ride either! For the next 4.5 miles you will be following the route of a flume (an old water system), originally developed in the 1870s to deliver water around the ridge to help transport logs and water to Virginia City. In places you will still see the pipes which replaced the original wooden flume. Be careful – they can be slippery at times. Plan on enough time to enjoy the views along the way, and if you like to take pictures bring along a camera. This is the place to take unbelievable photos of your friends riding along rugged granite walls with Lake Tahoe and the surrounding mountains in the background.

10.6 miles (4.5 miles of single track later!) – The Flume Trail ends at Tunnel Creek Road. The road to the left continues down 3 miles to Hidden Beach on Highway 28. (This ride can also be started from Hidden Beach, but the parking is very limited here). Just below this spot, down Tunnel Creek Road, are the remains of a tunnel that was blasted 4,000 feet through the mountains to the eastern side; water was transported through it by another series of flumes. To continue on the loop ride, turn right and ride up to the top of the ridge. 11.1 miles – The road to Twin Lakes takes off to the right. The Lakes are about a half mile away. Continue straight, or detour to the lakes before continuing on. 11.8 miles (0.7 mile past Twin Lakes sign) – While you are heading down the dirt road, look to your right for another section of rideable Flume Trail. The most enjoyable way is to turn right and continue along the flume, so look carefully. If you miss this turn, don't worry; continue down the road and take the next main road to the right. It will take you past the "Red House" and connect again with the Flume Trail. (The Red House is one of the old flume tender's houses built in 1910.)

Follow the Flume Trail as it contours around the east side of the Carson Range. Watch out for downed trees. Some of them you can ride over, others you can ride under, and some you will have to portage around. 14.2 miles – The Flume Trail ends at a small diversion dam. Carefully walk across or around the dam and continue up to the main road. Turn right. 14.7 miles – Turn right on Forest Road (504) that soon crosses Franktown Creek. If you need water, get it here. (Be sure to filter or treat the water.) The next section is a one-mile uphill that is mostly in the sun. Take a rest if you need it, then begin the climb to the top of the ridge. 15.9 miles – You have reached the top! Continue on out the ridge.

16.3 miles – The road forks. Although it may seem like it is time to go downhill, continue straight ahead. After a bit more ridge riding, the road quickly descends to Marlette Lake. 19 miles – You are now back at Marlette Lake and have completed the Loop part of the ride. Turn left at the intersection following the signs back to Spooner Summit. After a short climb, it's time for 4 miles of downhill. This section can get quite wild – sand seems to be in all the turns! Be sure to watch out for hikers, horseback riders and other cyclists. *Stay on the right side of the road and control your speed at all times.* 23 miles. Back to Spooner Lake and your car.

Ride #3 - Hobart Reservoir Loop

Level of Difficulty: Strong beginner to intermediate level ride, all on dirt roads.
Mileage: 20 miles.
Elevation: 7,000 ft. to 8,300 ft.

The Ride: 0.0 mile – From Spooner Lake ride north on the road to Marlette Lake, following the directions in Ride #1. 4.8 miles – When you reach the lake turn right and ride along the southeast shore. (The Flume Loop takes a left here). The road to Hobart Reservoir climbs a bit, follows the ridge line and descends the eastern side into a meadow and across Franktown Creek. 7.5 miles – Turn right and continue 0.5 mile to Hobart Reservoir. Hobart Reservoir is the main water supply for Virginia City, Silver City, Gold Hill and parts of Carson City, amazing when you you look on the map to see just how far away Virginia City is!

8.6 miles – Stay to the right. 0.3 mile farther, stay right again. The two roads you pass are the eastern access routes to this area if you are coming from Carson City or the Washoe Lake area. Continue on Forest Road 506, which turns west and begins to climb over Carson Ridge. 13.0 miles – After a short downhill you return to the road you started on. Turn left and ride down the hill to Marlette Lake. 14.8 miles – At Marlette Lake turn left, ride up the hill, then enjoy the downhill back to your car. **Caution:** *Be sure to ride carefully down the hill! Be on the lookout for hikers, horseback riders, and other cyclists making their way up. The turns can be loose and sandy, so control your speed at all times!*

MT. ROSE HIGHWAY

To get to these rides, start from Incline Village and either ride or drive north on Highway 431. If you are staying in Incline Village, you may choose to ride your bike from town. If so, look off to the side of the road after you leave the subdivisions for the old Mt. Rose Highway; ride it instead of the new road.

Ride #4 - Ophir Creek Trail

Topo Maps: Mt. Rose 7.5 min., or Mt. Rose, NV 15 min. Ride starts at T17N, R19, Section 36.
Level of Difficulty: Good for beginners and young children. This is a pretty spot, with limited riding and is probably not worth a special trip. But if you are on your way to Reno, or you like little out-of-the-way spots where you can ride, picnic, hike and go fishing, give Ophir Creek a try. Ophir Creek looks small, but while it

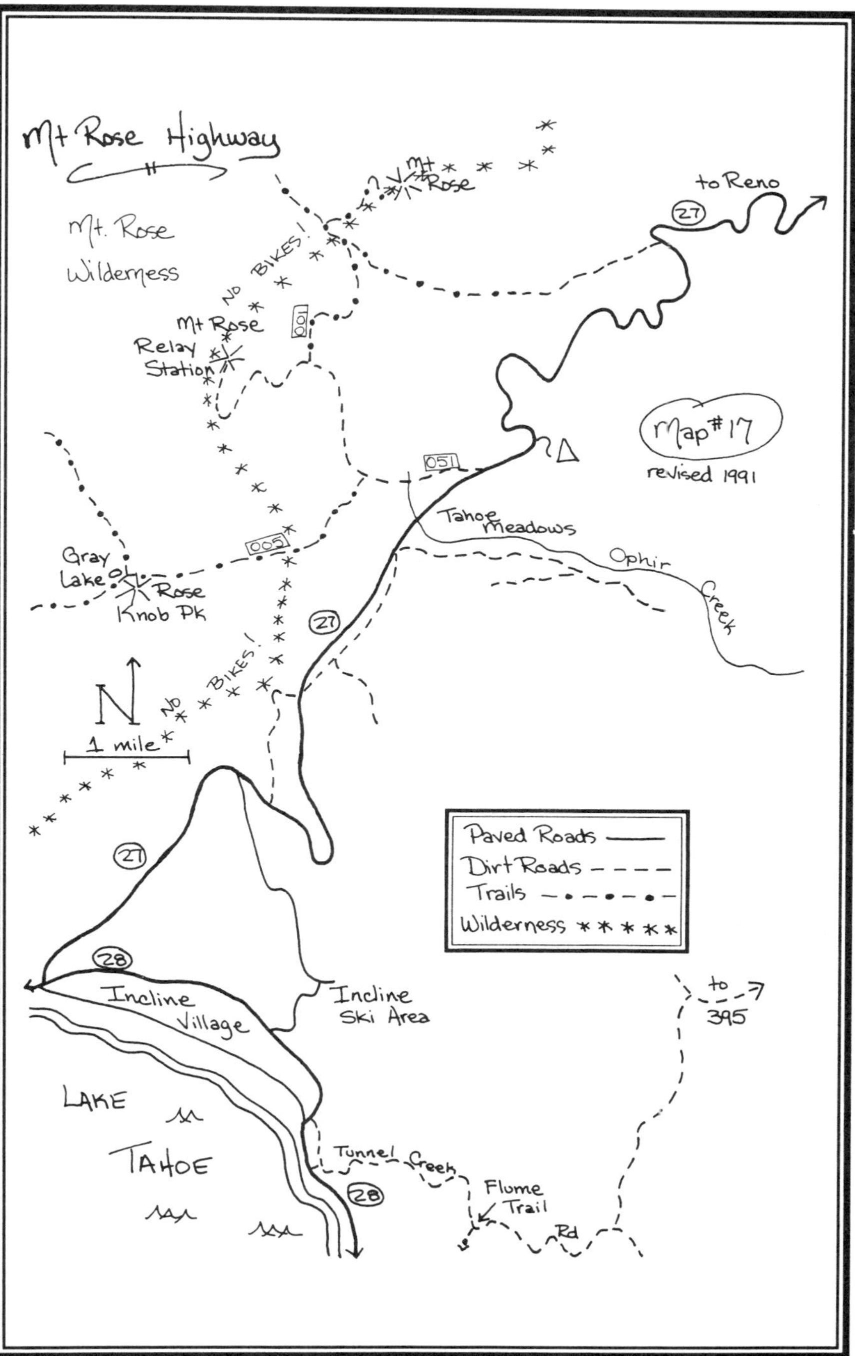

Mt Rose Highway
Mt. Rose Wilderness
NO BIKES!
Mt Rose
Mt Rose Relay Station
to Reno
27
100
Map #17
revised 1991
051
Tahoe Meadows
Ophir Creek
005
Gray Lake
Rose Knob Pk
27
NO BIKES!
N
1 mile
27
28
Incline Village
Incline Ski Area
to 395
Paved Roads
Dirt Roads
Trails
Wilderness
LAKE
TAHOE
Tunnel Creek
Flume Trail
Rd
28

is only two to three feet across, it is three feet deep with even deeper holes! People were fishing successfully while we were here, and the creek looks crystal clear.

Mileage: Ophir Creek Trail is 3 miles out and back; from Incline Village 17 miles.

Elevation: 8,500 ft. with very little elevation gain. If you choose to start this ride from Incline Village and ride up to the trail, the elevation gain will be from 6,240 feet to 8,500 feet.

Campgrounds: Mt. Rose Campground is located 10 miles up Highway 431 – almost to the summit. According to the Campground Host, this USFS campground is rarely full, except on the busiest weekends of the summer. The terrain is fairly barren, although there is a creek nearby.

Drive or ride up Highway 431, which travels northeast out of Incline Village 7.5 miles. Off to your right (east) is the Ophir Creek Trailhead sign. The trail is located on the edge of Tahoe Meadows, a large expanse with a winter parking area. If you come to the parking area you have gone too far, so head back to the edge of the meadow by the creek to find the trail. Park at the trailhead.

Follow the "trail" – really an old jeep road – out about a mile and a half. Several short out-and-back options are also available. This is a large winter recreation area with cross-country ski markers on many trees. Just before the road ends, you will see another road taking off down a drainage. This old 4-wheel drive road turns into a motorcycle trail and then ends up at Incline Village Ski Resort. If you decide to follow this down, please obey all signs and stay on the trail – you are travelling through private land. A short distance past Incline Ski Area, you reach a large intersection where three roads meet. Turn right. Follow this road back to Highway 431, find the old Mt. Rose Highway, and ride back up to your car or continue straight ahead to Incline Village.

Ride #5 - Mt. Rose Relay Station

Level of Difficulty: Advanced ride, due to the elevation and lack of shade.

Elevation: 8,800 ft. to 10,160 ft.

Mileage: 8 miles out and back.

Water: None available; carry all that you will need.

Seasons: Mid-June through October. Avoid the middle of the summer; there is no shade on this ride.

This ride takes you to the top of a 10,166 foot peak with a Relay Station (Radio Repeater and Microwave Station) at the top. Don't be fooled by the low mileage! This is a tough climb, similar to riding up to fire lookouts.

Driving northeast on Highway 431 from Incline Village, you'll see a gated road 1 mile past Tahoe Meadows on the left. Park here, or drive up to Mt. Rose summit to park.

The Ride: 0.0 mile – Ride your bike out the 4-wheel drive road marked Forest Road 051. Stay on the main road that climbs up and around a ridge, then turns north into a canyon. 2.2 miles. (*Note:* At this point, the trail to the left goes to Gray

Lake; the trail to the right goes to Mt. Rose. Although you may hike to either of these areas, *your bike is not allowed in the Wilderness.*) Continue on to the relay station. The road begins to get very steep as you climb the final 80 ft. to the top. 3.9 miles – You're at the top now where you have a spectacular 360° view. When you have enjoyed the view retrace the route back to your car.

Outdoor Books from
Fine Edge Productions

Mountain Biking the High Sierra

Guide 1	Owens Valley and Inyo County, Second Edition	$8.95
Guide 2	Mammoth Lakes and Mono County, Second Edition	$8.95
Guide 3A	Lake Tahoe South, Second Edition	$8.95
Guide 3B	Lake Tahoe North, Second Edition	$8.95

Mountain Biking the Coast Range

Guide 4	Ventura County and the Sespe, Second Edition	$8.95
Guide 5	Santa Barbara County, Second Edition	$8.95
Guide 7	Santa Monica Mountains	$8.95
Guide 8	Saugus District of the Angeles N.F. with Mt. Pinos	$8.95
Guide 9	San Gabriel Mountains, Angeles N.F.	$8.95

Mountain Biking Maps (topographical)

North Lake Tahoe Basin Recreation Map, w/profiles & trail descriptions	$8.95
South Lake Tahoe Basin Recreation Map, w/profiles & trail descriptions	$8.95
San Gabriel Mountains — West; includes Verdugo Mountains	$8.95
Excelsior District, Tahoe N.F., Lake Tahoe Region, Hwy. 80	$6.95
Crystal Basin, Eldorado N.F., Lake Tahoe Region, Hwy. 50	$6.95
Moab, Utah, Slick Rock	$5.95

Also available:

Favorite Pedal Tours of Northern California	$12.95
Ski Touring the Eastern High Sierra	$8.95
Beginning and Intermediate Cross-Country Day Trips	
Exploring California's Channel Islands, an Artist's View	$6.95

Additional books and maps in process.

For current titles and prices, please send SASE.

To order any of these items see your local dealer or send
your check to Fine Edge Productions at the address below.
Please include $2.00 for shipping. California residents add sales tax.

Fine Edge Productions, Route 2, Box 303, Bishop, California 93514